comes with

furniture and people

charlotte matthews

Black Rose Writing | Texas

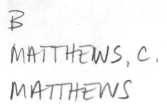

B
MATTHEWS, C.
MATTHEWS

First printing

Some names and identifying details may have been changed to protect the privacy of individuals.

ISBN: 978-1-68433-397-4
PUBLISHED BY BLACK ROSE WRITING
www.blackrosewriting.com

Printed in the United States of America
Suggested Retail Price (SRP) $16.95

Comes With Furniture and People is printed in Caslon

*The final word count for this book may not match your standard expectation versus the final page count. In an effort to reduce paper usage and energy costs, Black Rose Writing, as a planet-friendly publisher, does its best to eliminate unnecessary waste without lessening your reading experience.

You can change a person's life by saying just one thing, just once.

This book is for all the people who helped me find a path.
It is also for Albert who believes, for Emma who is present,
and for Garland who gladdens.

It is in memory of my mother, Joan Carson Matthews.

comes with
furniture and people

There is no greater agony than bearing an untold story inside you.
~Maya Angelou

The thought of touching my mother startles me to this day. Ours was a business relationship. Her job: make sure I was clothed and fed. Mine: need as little as possible. I'd stand in awe as my best friend's mother brushed my hair, nimbly working out knots beneath a fan that sucked the smell of bacon from their tiled kitchen. But once a year, on the fourth of July, my mother, my brother and I would stand in front of her bathroom window and watch fireworks flower over the Washington Monument. For a spell of time, we'd hold our breath while pillars of color cascaded three miles away. I remember how calm she smelled, a serene mixture of soap and copper and leaves. The fanfare over, we'd return to our lives, our separate selves. So rare were the occasions of our physical proximity we came away perplexed like we'd done something forbidden.

What my mother did when she left the house remains a mystery. There was proof she'd visited the library and gone to the Safeway. But the rest of her day was as remote as she was. My best guess is she stayed away as long as she possibly could, driving down McArthur Boulevard or across Chain Bridge into Virginia where she'd contemplate the water as it sloshed over rocks in the Potomac far below. Sometimes she must have simply parked and read or closed her eyes, hands resting on the steering wheel.

I kept careful tabs on my mother's reading. One week it might be Mary Renault's *Alexander Trilogy*, the next: Robert Graves' *Goodbye to All That*. The weeks she checked out a Barbara Pym or Agatha Christie, her reading spilled late into the night. She spent most of her time reading: in the afternoon on the paisley love seat in the sitting room. At dusk downstairs in the living room, head supported by the side of her wing chair, a glass of tonic water and Angostura Bitters sweating on the marble-topped table beside her.

At exactly 7:15 we ate dinner. Even though it was just the three of us, she'd ring the bell, a wooden-handled thing with a tinny sound. That meant Clark and I were to come downstairs so we could sit at the dining room table and eat Stouffer's followed by cherry Jell-O with two Pepperidge Farm gingerbread cookies.

This was all after my father left. Following that, Mommy established that he would never cross the threshold of the house again. And she took to listening incessantly to Scott Joplin. On the eight-track: The Maple Leaf Rag and The Entertainer, every day for hours at a time. The first week I thought she was trying to cheer herself up, but soon I understood that frenzied cadence had another purpose. Disquieting and alarming, it was the soundtrack to her current life.

When Mommy talked on the phone, which was almost never, I'd pace the tiles trying to figure out what mattered to her. I wanted to overhear clues about what she was thinking, what she felt, what she would not tell me on her own. *Only white ones*, I'd instruct myself. *Do not step an inch on a black tile, or something else bad will happen.* In the hallway was a radiator with a star-patterned, white metal cover. There sat a silver tray with her married initials, JCM, a wedding gift. That is where the car keys went. It was also where my father would place his cufflinks after he took off his jacket, tie, and suspenders. Before he left us for another woman. Before he died eighteen months later.

My mother talked to herself as if she were someone else, employing the third person voice: *Good morning, Joan. Today is Tuesday, February the 25th. Yes, it is. And you need to get the oil changed in the car. Do that before the snow comes this afternoon.* Oddly, it was this talk that supplied the greatest comfort of my childhood. It remains one of the most intimate things I can imagine: lying in bed, hearing my mother's voice parse out the day. Each morning, and in the exact same fashion, she'd read aloud the day's page of her engagement book, meticulously, as if giving dictation. And each evening, after dinner, she'd go back through the day, saying check to establish she'd completed a task: *change oil in car—check.*

The engagement books were leather and black, and in December we'd drive to Sherman's Engraving and Stationery off DuPont Circle to secure one for the next calendar year. Side by side, she'd note obligations as well as events. *April 4, 1968: 10:00: hair appointment; 7:00: Martin Luther King, Jr. is shot.* Unlike all the other days, for that one, I can fill in the missing emotions. Here they are in the form of a poem.

Epoxy

> *My spell check honorably refused to*
> *recognize the word nigger.*
> Ellen Bryant Voigt

I am three when King is shot,
and riots erupt in the city a
ll around. When the phone rings
my mother goes to the hallway,
then slams the receiver down
mid-call. From the sink
she picks up a bar of Ivory
soap and holds it right next
to my face where it smells so clean.
But she is shaking and gritting her
teeth. If I ever, ever say the word,
she will watch as I eat
that bar right down. She will
watch, unflinching, as I get sick,
sick as she feels in that moment.

You might be dubious that a three-
year-old would remember an
incident so crisply. But the smell of
Ivory soap, that white, white soap,
brings this moment right back to
me. I can still see her, my mother,
standing in front of my high chair in
her housedress. I can hear her
saying those words with such
ferocity. She meant what she said.
She always did.

laundromats

My mother was drawn to pragmatic people and practical places, establishments with a straightforward purpose. She had absolutely no tolerance for frivolity. Nail salons were strictly off limits. As were coffee shops. *You can make your own coffee at home for far less money,* she'd say. A Saturday outing might include a trip to Dalton's Hardware, to the Georgetown branch of the public library and to Brown's Cleaners. That night she'd check off her list that she'd gotten a new washer for the dripping faucet in the powder room, borrowed a book on Egyptian pharaohs and picked up the bedspread she'd brought in the previous Saturday. And while I don't remember us ever going to one, I suspect she would have been wholeheartedly in favor of laundromats. Because she liked to accomplish things. Because it gave her a sense of relief to get things done.

It's not only the warmth of so many dryers all in a row that I relish. I also like how every person in the building is doing something quite private (washing underwear and pillowcases and socks) in public and in unison, a kind of chorus. We are all in this together, every last one of us, for a discreet amount of time with a definite purpose. We've brought what is sullied, what is dirty, in hopes of changing all that. And here in this low-slung building, we have to wait. Also, I admire how the largest machines can sustain heavy duty loads. And how about those two words together: heavy duty? Pretty great.

Yesterday at Suds, sitting in the chair beside me reading *Newsweek* is a man who seems nothing less than the spitting image of Joe Early, the man who drove my school bus for ten years. Joe's authority grew the day a sedan barreled past the bus's blinking lights, and he launched a tire jack straight through that Volare's back window. Everything stilled, the filaments of rear window defrosters waving, metallic spider webs in November's air, metronome cadence of bus lights clicking. Because Joe made the littler kids sit up front and because the ride lasted 30 minutes, I'd clocked many an hour staring at the back of Joe's neck. There was a crease in it, a fold of skin, supple and dark. I had the strongest urge to wedge a pencil in it horizontally, to somehow get that close to him.

The day after the tire jack incident, my father died suddenly and at work. He had a heart attack, a quiet one, in his chair. The news came in the form of a phone call: my father's chin had dropped to his chest, what must have looked like a cat nap. The next morning, I got up, got dressed and went to school. Because that is what I did during the week. And because Joe would be waiting for me at the bus stop. And he was a man I could trust, day in and day out, to pick me up and take me home.

I kept the fact of my father's death to myself all the way until third period Latin when I asked our teacher, Imogen Rose, if I could skip the conjugation quiz because my father had died the night before. The look on her face was such a peculiar mixture of disbelief and horror I can replicate it to this day. To get the full impact, one must understand just how Mrs. Rose ran her classroom. If one of us yawned, we were to leave the room and take a brisk lap around the building's exterior, sleet of February no consideration. *Yawning means one is in need of oxygen*, she established on the first day of each term when she spelled out the rules. When she entered the room, we stood up until she lifted her right index finger in the manner of an orchestra conductor. This meant we were to sit back down. The day I lengthened my school uniform so that it came all the way to my ankles to appear hippy-ish, the note she sent home read, *Charlotte's uniform unacceptable, appears as if she is in a ditch, please hem.*

Before I was old enough to go to school, I spent most of my time on a closed-in porch just off my bedroom pretending to be a teacher. When my current students ask me how long I've been at this trade, it's hard not to include those years. My porch classroom was even fully equipped: a chalkboard, dolls for students, black and white composition books, a xylophone. It is such a fond memory and is, I think, one of the many reasons I love teaching. I can be back in that sunny room with its mustard colored rug and cantilevered windows. I can be eight all over again.

Next to my writing desk is a photograph of Christmas morning. I look to be four, which makes Clark nine. We are standing in front of the fireplace, three empty red stockings hanging glumly over the fire screen. Mommy is stooping so as to be low, down at my level. Her left-hand cradles a doll who is half my size. She is teaching me how to support a baby's head. She is emphasizing the importance of paying attention to the fontinelles. If only she knew how dutifully I remember that lesson. She taught me that to swaddle an infant properly you must first place the baby in the center of the blanket, then tuck in the blanket's left side, followed by the bottom, and lastly the right. You make it compact, a tight, snug bundle.

Broken bones stitch back together on their own. While Mommy mended, while she sewed on a button or hemmed my school uniform, I would stitch up imaginary cuts on my stuffed animals. Sometimes I would sew two animals together: an arm to an arm, a hoof to a paw, so they would not lose each other, so they could be together in a permanent kind of way. It is, of course, what I wanted for my mother and me. Though I knew, even then, that would never happen. When my friend Marianne said to me one day that *to be a child is to be adrift in strangeness*, she put words to what I'd felt all along. I was unanchored in a sea of discord.

Tuesdays and Sundays at noon the bells of the Washington National Cathedral peal for a full forty-five minutes. This requires 1260 bell changes and is a sound so glorious I was surprised something like that could find its way into our house. You heard it best in the front hallway, a room with a tiled floor, so the notes resonated all the more. Uncharacteristically, one weekend my mother took a workshop from the band of ringers. There she was pulling a rope to engage the clapper on a bell that weighed two thousand pounds. There she was making the sound we relished unequivocally.

Each Halloween, we'd disconnect the doorbell. Outside, all the ghosts and princesses traipsed up the stairs through oak leaves only to be met by silence.

We kept the lights out, too, to make it seem as if we weren't home. Christmases, we ate at the neighborhood Chinese restaurant, the one place open. This was our job on holidays: avoid them at all costs. And it is a lesson that has, for better or worse, stayed with me all these years When a holiday approaches, I brace myself, knowing the hard place inside of me will grow bigger, sponge sea creature you set in a bowl of water until it expands to 100 times its original size.

Christmas mornings the Cathedral televised its services all over the nation. The boys' soprano voices called to me, so I'd walk the two blocks to stand under the flying buttresses where I'd close my eyes and listen to that transcendent sound. Clark and Mommy watched the service from the upstairs sitting room. Walking back, I'd think how we'd heard the same thing, but from perspectives. I'd think how much of life is like this.

guileless as elmer's glue

·————————►·

I grew up without guesswork about where we were going to live or what we were going to eat. The rotation of Stouffer's meals went something like this: Monday: turkey tetrazzini; Tuesday: stuffed bell peppers; Wednesday: creamed chipped beef; Thursday: chicken pot pie; Friday: lasagna. I don't remember the weekend meals much, though we would occasionally go out to eat. And I was as certain as a person could be that we would never move. That brick house on Garfield Street with its slate roof and radiator heat was part of my mother. She embodied it. There was simply no place else for her to reside.

How I knew my mother had something incurable is hard to say, except we have all witnessed how a dog senses a thunderstorm long before the rest of us. That's the best way to explain it. My entire childhood, I felt something menacing burgeoning in her, something slow growing, taking over her body. She was a stately, modest woman, and I'd never seen her in anything other than pants suits and house dresses, occasionally a flannel nightgown. Still, I knew that underneath those garments, something had gone irreparably wrong. And when it grew worse, became bigger, overtook her all the way—who would take care of me then?

And I was right. The year after leukemia cells got the best of her, *The*

Washington Post ran a front-page story: photographs of the contaminated soil she'd played in as a kid, pictures of the very street in Spring Valley she lived on cordoned off, her house, her lawn, on the front page of The Post. Turns out, her neighborhood had been a bomb testing ground during World War I. The Army Corps of Engineers has proclaimed the area uninhabitable. As I write this, they are conducting a clean-up of a one-mile wide swath of northwest Washington.

I still have my mother's address book, a blue three-inch hardback I remember buying together on one of our rare outings. She entered names with a black flair pen in her flawless, left-handed script. Whenever someone moved, she marked through the old address and wrote the new one below it. If someone died, she blacked out the most recent address, then wrote the date of death. Even though much of the book had cross-throughs, she refused to buy another. I can understand why.

I wonder about the van driver who drove my mother's body from the hospital to the funeral home. It was January, icy and cold. Was he listening to the news? Was she smoking a Salem Light? Did he know what cargo he had? When Gauler's Funeral Home told us we needed to confirm the body as hers, Clark stood up without pause. Four minutes later, when he came back to the conference room where we were meeting with the funeral home director, his face revealed nothing of what he had just seen: our mother, dead under a white sheet, about to be burnt up. I've never asked my brother about it, but my gratitude for his taking on that task will never, ever fade.

Yesterday my students and I set out to compile a list of agreed-upon facts: oil floats on water, if you touch its whiskers a cat will blink, the earth is not flat, pearls melt in vinegar. But the exercise got tricky real quick. We all had to agree it was an agreed upon fact. How long do houseflies live? Do elephants cry? Does time speed up when you get older?

In Hindi, there is a phrase: *to me, your memory comes*. It is the same as our saying *I miss you*. Hindus use it to address the living. I employ it for the dead. My mother's memory comes to me. I miss her. Because she was an expert at staying distant in real life (agreed upon fact) now that she's gone, I miss her in a way that does not fade, guileless and dependable as Elmer's Glue. Sometimes I miss my mother so much she turns into the woman on the city bus, the stranger carrying a bag stuffed with cans of cat food. She becomes the single sound I can hear, all my attention has room for. When I got the news of her death, I turned into someone else, and for a very long time—a shocking alchemy. I became a motherless daughter. I became an orphan.

My train is rolling slowly north, rural Virginia countryside. In the town of

Orange, I see into shop windows, the tracks mere feet from Main Street. On one corner, a man exuberantly waves a brown paper bag at the passing train. The passenger seated across the aisle from me does not open the book that's perched on his lap—but I don't really expect him to. He looks like he's just heard bad news, the kind you keep on hearing long after the words have been said. The kind that hangs in the air, stagnant and suffocating. It reminds me that there is no good way to get such news, and that there is no wrong way to mourn.

On the train, I read a novel, translated from Italian, entitled *The Days of Abandonment*. Like most books I love, it's hard to say what it's about. There's regret and loneliness, there's suspicion and disfigurement. And there's this sentence: *we carry in our head until we die the living and the dead*. My mother, though she's been dead for two decades, peoples my head as much as—no, far more than—living people I see every day. There she is in her sitting room, as real to me as these words, as real as paprika.

the ganz swan

Because radiators are crucial to this story, I'll offer a few more details. There was a boiler in the basement, and when the hot water rose up through the pipes, the entire house clanged. It was an elemental sound, sublime and affirming: *clang, clang clang*, brass grommet hitting a flagpole. I'd stand in my bedroom with my legs pressed up again the radiator, absorbing its heat. I'd tell myself I was in training to be a spy. My view out the window was onto a key intersection in our nation's capital, and I'd watched the presidential motorcade pass by many a time, the unmarked cars, the ones with an inconspicuous blue light on the dash. I'd make a list of all the things I haven't yet done. I'd list all the places I wanted to travel. I'd tell myself *it's okay, this is a normal childhood, this expanse, this nothingness.*

My view onto the corner of Cleveland Avenue and Garfield Street also provided the opportunity to watch the light change. Sometimes I would count the seconds, other times I held my breath the entire length of the yellow light, the shortest one. When it rained, the colors ricocheted off the wet, black street. I'd stand there until my legs, beneath my corduroy pants, tingled and I had to step back a few inches. This was my evening ritual, every day for all the years of my growing up. Tuesdays in winter my mother bled the furnace, opened a spigot on it, so the dirty water flowed into a bucket. Then she'd put in a bit of fresh water. It was like she was giving the house, which itself was a presence, a transfusion. She was keeping it alive.

Even though she had few friends, my mother read the obituaries faithfully and exhaustively. I'm pretty sure it's the real reason she took the paper. Occasionally she'd break the breakfast table silence: *Oh, John Oliphant died. I dated him in tenth grade. He was dreamy. Wonder what happened?* And, this would be the first I'd heard of this person. Another day she might say to the air in the room, as much as she would to me, *Well now, look at that, Mr. Pilkington stayed working for the World Bank up until the day he died. I could have betted on that, hard worker that he was.* Looking back, I understand that it was not until death that she allowed herself to admit she cared for someone.

So it is stupefying to think of how my mother wished to die: alone, without her children even knowing it. While I've cataloged her death obtusely in poems, it seems important to tell the story outright, start to end. Here it is. During our weekly Wednesday phone call, I tell her I am pregnant, and she tells me she is not feeling well, says her doctors are going to run some tests on her. So focused on my news, I am not tuned in enough to recognize that what she has said is serious. Very serious. And she intentionally leaves out the fact that she is scheduled to meet her hematologist at the hospital the very next day. She leaves out the fact that she is being admitted to the hospital and that her white blood cell count is 215,000.

She must have known this was the end. Why else would she have asked our neighbor to drive her to Sibley Hospital? So her car would remain at home. So it wouldn't sit untended, accruing fines, in a hospital parking garage after she died. So Clark and I would have one less thing to deal with. She also asked that neighbor, Mary Lela, not to tell Clark or me that she was being admitted. She asked it be a secret. And I'll never know the reason. Did she not want the attention? Did she hope to not disrupt our lives? Did she think she should keep the stiff upper lip until the end? I don't know. And Mary Lela did wait 24 hours before she told us, calling late on Sunday night.

I drove as fast as I could from Charlottesville, and Clark and she and I had 40 hours together. And there were some stunning moments. The second day, Mommy's nurse suggested that a Swan Ganz catheter might make her more comfortable. By that point, she was pretty much gone, what the medical community calls non compos mentis or of unsound mind. But still, I decided to let this decision be hers. I pulled my chair as close as I could to the side of the hospital bed. But that put me too low. So, I stood and asked her: *Mommy, would you like to have a Swan Ganz catheter?* It sounded the way I might have asked if she'd care for some extra cream in her coffee or some freshly grated parmesan cheese on her lasagna.

Well, here's the thing: she lifted the oxygen mask a few inches from her face and answered in a stronger voice than I'd heard for hours, *that would be absolutely lovely.* It must have been the name of the catheter that delighted her. I imagine her envisioning a swan floating on a cold New England lake, a Ganz swan, not the usual pristine white one. My mother's swan would be metal grey, quite the elegant fellow. In her morphine haze, she was still so enamored with words and their sounds that she invented a new breed of water bird. So, into the large needle's eye, the nurse maneuvered navy-blue thread. Then he sewed in the catheter oh so carefully as if this would be something that would last a long time, not the 24 hours she had left to live. The indebtedness I feel for how he treated my mother knows no bounds. I will revere that nurse and his precise, dark hands forever.

The night nurse who'd wheeled her from the ICU to the step-down unit where she died reported that Mommy was singing opera to herself the whole way. She couldn't make out which opera, but my mother was most definitely singing behind her oxygen mask. I like envisioning that. There she is singing La Traviata as the elevator clicks between floors.

In what was the last full conversation I had with her, I asked if she would like me to read her Peter Taylor's *A Summons to Memphis*, a book she loved. She lifted the oxygen mask to establish, *you know I've read all of his books a dozen times already. No thank you.* It was neither mean nor dismissive. It was matter of fact, just like her.

Was my mother ready to die? The neighbor who drove her to the hospital, Mary Lela, chose to read John Mansfield's *Sea-Fever* at the funeral. That poem's hope for *quiet sleep and a sweet dream when the long trick's over* seems to point to the fact that just maybe she was. The poem also has these lines: *I must go down to the seas again, to the lonely sea and sky, and all I ask is a tall ship and a star to steer her by.* That encapsulates my mother so well, particularly that loneliness. And though I never saw her in any water myself, I suspect she had reverence for the ocean, for its power and its majesty, for what it establishes about our small humanness. She understood that all too well.

A friend of mine, a fellow Quaker, wrote me the following condolence letter: *Your absence today from midweek worship was unexplained until the meeting broke, and then I learned that your mother had suddenly closed her life.* That is the most accurate way to explain it. She closed her life. She was in control. She did things her own way.

I stayed at her house for the two days following her death, stayed there with the yellow lab she loved so much: Maggie, Maggie May. Well, I stayed during the day but could not bear to spend the night. She died early on Tuesday morning, and when the mail came through the front door slot on Wednesday, I was greeted by my own handwriting on a powder blue envelope. I had written her a letter she would never receive. In it, I told her about my students and how we were reading Faulkner, how we were picking our way through it the way you cross a creek, finding stepping stones, wobbling a bit here and there. And I'd described the herd of cows I passed on my morning run, how I'd seen a calf, newly born, steaming on top of a bale of hay surrounded by ice and snow, his mother licking him clean. I told her I would see her soon, which I thought I would.

hindsight bias

Yesterday, outside Kroger, a little girl was riding a plastic horse her mother had put fifty cents into to make it rock and play *It's a Small World After All*. The joy in that girl's face was enough to make you love most anything. It was as if this was the moment she'd been waiting these seven long years to live. I, like the girl, felt a sudden and unexplainable current of exultation. I also felt a jolt of recognition recalling that is the exact song the Good Humor truck would play as it wove through the alleys of my childhood: *it's a small, small world.*

My students this semester, a lot of them engineers, are kind and earnest and smart. On the second day of class, Kelsi nonchalantly used the term hindsight bias. When I asked her for examples, she looked at me with her enviably placid, brown eyes: *that we should have known the car needed new brakes. That the elderly man, Robert, who died of pneumonia, should have gotten a flu shot.* Hindsight bias is the fact that events seem more predictable after they have happened.

For some reason, it made me remember the interpreter at Nelson Mandela's funeral. Instead of signing what was being spoken, his hand signals spelled out shrimp and rocking horses. When confronted and reprimanded for this, he said he'd seen angels on his way into the stadium. Hindsight bias: maybe he was right, maybe there were no words to sum up such a man as

Mandela, maybe flapping one's arms was the ideal way to pay tribute, to wave goodbye to a man who spent more than a quarter of his life in prison for resolutely opposing a policy of racial discrimination.

More often than not, even in the game of hide and go seek, children want to be found, hearts racing as they wait for the counting to end—*5, 4, 3, 2, 1, ready or not here I come*—to hear footsteps nearing the linen closet door where they are hiding under stacks of fitted sheets. There is such a spectacular urgency to it all. Even now, in what I hope is the middle of my life, I sometimes find the need to run away: to the woods or the field behind the house. I do it most often in autumn when the cold begins to set in. Do I want to be found? I think so, but part of me remains unsure.

At random times, students I've taught over the past three decades pop up in my personal viewfinder, one by one, with a snippet about their lives, the little I know of them outside of class. John was a tillerman during his career as a firefighter. His job was to steer the rear wheels and maneuver the engine through narrow city streets. Unprotected in the rear cab, he said the worst part was getting blasted by all that wind in his face, wind on cold days, wind and sleet and rain. Another student, Sarah, exclusively ate green items for lunch: lima beans, lettuce, pistachios. She would sit in the hallway's wide windowsill and look out at the grass. Even her hair was green. I wonder where she is now. Esther was part of a triplet, and her sisters, Hanna and Naomi looked so much like her they could have easily attended class for one another, and I would not have known the difference.

But let me return to the tillerman because the first thing I think of when I hear the word tillerman is the Cat Stevens' *Tea for the Tillerman*, a decidedly popular album in the 70's and early 80's. And this makes me wonder how in the world the dude steering the back half of a long truck would be able to drink the tea he was proffered—if that's what he drinks anyway. I'm envisioning more a Mountain Dew guy for the one steerling that treacherous vehicle, or maybe if the ride's extraordinarily cold, black coffee. But I love that Cat Stevens album, and I respect my student, so I'll just leave this parcel as it is.

A few months ago, a dog headed for Kansas ended up in Japan. Yup, it's true. I suppose there is a slant rhyme to it: Kansas, Japan. And I suspect it must have had to do with transcription. But envision, just for a moment, being that dog. You're looking forward to the slower pace of farm life, running through the wheat fields, snoozing under the front porch, but lo and behold, there you find yourself in the Kyoto airport, and no one says anything you even vaguely recognize: No *good dog*, no treat, no walk. Talk about a rude awakening.

I was thinking of all this when I got stuck in the service elevator recently at a literary conference. If you've ever been to one of these events, or pretty much any conference where people with shared ideas glom together, you know it gets claustrophobic and weird pretty darn fast. By day two, my head was swirling, so instead of boarding the elevator meant for guests, I got on the one the custodial staff use, the one with a secret door in the back. And what I noticed first off was that there was no elevator inspector's report mounted under cheap plastic just above the buttons of numbered floors. I like it most when you get the photograph of the mayor or governor. And then I savor the handwriting: *inspected by Bernard L. Folk, January 11, 2019*. It makes it all seems pretty safe. Well, I'll tell you now, the service elevator had nothing of that. No inspection. No cool picture of kids "talking" with Styrofoam cups over a distance. No promises of hot cookies. It was terrifically disorienting.

I just gained a week. A good bit better than gaining a pound, which I seem to do lately by merely looking at food. But I digress. Today, I showed up for appointments, one a meeting with a colleague, another a luncheon, a full week early, this Thursday rather than next. Yup, and I felt the opposite of embarrassment, felt simultaneously revved up and utterly confused. Plus, I don't believe in embarrassment. It is a futile emotion. Regret, that's another thing entirely. You can't undo regret. I regret so many things, so many tarnished friendships, so many unkind words. But embarrassment: I just cannot let that one in.

comes with furniture and people

My mother is standing in the doorway of her bedroom. Then she turns to the bureau to fold socks. She has them divided by color, so all she needs to do is match them up, pair them. It's clear she enjoys this task, something to accomplish and check off the list she keeps stored in her head.

But this is not actually happening right now. Not in the real world. It's just that I want it to be. She's been dead for two decades, and I want so badly to be able to tell her about Emma and Garland, my children, grandchildren she never met. I want her to know them, and they her. I've inundated Emma with stories about her grandmother because she is uncannily like her, almost a replica. And Emma was born eight months to the day after my mother's death. January 20, 1998: Mommy died: September 20, 1998: Emma was born. What are the chances of that? I'll tell her how Mommy would perch on the loveseat reading Agatha Christie, solving the mystery under her breath, audible to no one but me. Outside trees would scrape their voices into the wind.

At 20, Emma already embodies the stoicism and assuredness of my mother. They would understand each other. There they are at Panda Garden ordering spring rolls and wonton soup, inventing new lives for patrons at the other tables under their breaths. This outing will be fodder enough for them to hold onto the entire rest of the day. They'll go home and wonder out loud together why the man with the topcoat and his companion were not talking to each other. Then they'll get to the looming question of why in the world the man was wearing a topcoat in the first place. They would respect each other for what they said, but even more for what they each left unsaid.

Mommy believed that there were three levels of discourse: lowest (so to her the least intellectual and least interesting): things, acquisitions, what you own or want to buy; middle level: people. It's how she explained the reason we human beings like to gossip. We are, by our natures, enthralled with the goings-on of our own species, particularly if the behavior is outside of accepted norms. And the highest level of talk: ideas, philosophy. I think that's why she loved myths so ardently. Myths that warn as well as promise, myths that lament as much as celebrate, suited her so well. They were more reliable than outright faith. She tussled her whole life with believing in God. It was too turbulent for her. But I won't say much more about that because we don't want it to end up with moths and rust.

Much of what my mother loved I also love. It works that way, like osmosis. She took stock of what I saw and felt. She curated it. In her sitting room, where all important decisions were made, she taught me that in England cattails are called bulrushes. That on Good Friday in 1930, the BBC aired no news. They played piano music the whole day long. I suspect she found that quite fitting and lovely, though she never confessed to it. And she wondrously taught me—by writing it out in red flair pen on a legal pad—that an anagram is a sentence containing every letter in the language: *The quick brown fox jumps over the lazy dog.* She whistled as she watched me let that one sink in.

I don't remember what my father looked like. But I can provide quite a few details about all of our dogs. When I was born, my parents still had Egore, the dachshund they'd gotten in Germany on their honeymoon. Then, there was a Scottie named Fergus and another named Dunstan, perfect names. Then a pug called Smudge which fit his smashed-in face superbly. We had a stray named Waif and a long-haired German Shepherd: Agatha. That is when my mother got in the groove of entitling all the dogs with "A" names: Agatha the shepherd, Asia the overweight Doberman Pincher, and Annie the sweet yellow lab.

Reading the local paper, I come upon a listing for a dollhouse. The ad states that it comes with furniture and people. Take a moment to think that one through. Comes with furniture and people. In a way, though, it is your house and it is mine. It's a description, albeit a brief one, of the places we live. Except we don't sell that way. The furniture and people move when our house goes up for sale. Mayflower Moving Company comes, or Three Guys with a Truck, and we and our possessions relocate, and different furniture and people move in.

But this dollhouse listing has them for sale altogether, a kind of package deal.

My grandfather made my mother a dollhouse. Its roof is kelly green, and the fake logs in the living room light up a wondrous garnet red. I love the thing but could never get anyone to play with it—except my brother. At seven, I did not understand that he was gay or that his husband would end up collecting vintage Barbie dolls, so I felt indebted to him each time he would choose to spend a few hours with me padding the miniature people up the stairs and making them talk in distinctive voices. He even went *up we go* as he moved their legs to escort them over the hall landing. The dollhouse was exquisitely furnished: oriental rugs, a Hoosier cabinet in the kitchen, four poster twin beds in the children's room, fleur-de-lis wallpaper.

How my grandfather must have labored over this project. I picture him painting the roof, hanging the miniature chandelier in the dining room. Because I've long thought that it is the little things that have the greatest impact, this dollhouse matters. It's over eighty years old. The doll, who is clearly the mother, has on an apron, and you can make out the yellow roses of its feed sack material. The hallway still has black and white parquet flooring. And it smells faintly of my own mother, a smell I love.

I like to envision her playing with it. She positions the mother doll in a chair reading (there were even centimeter sized books) beneath the floor lamp. She returns the copper pots to the Hoosier cabinet while humming *the bear's gone round the mountain, the bear's gone round the mountain*. And when she's done playing, she'll turn back the bedsheets and place the three children—two girls and a boy—in their respective beds oh so gingerly. She'll draw the shades: good night.

family night

Living catty-corner to a funeral home has its advantages. The same day *The Daily Progress* runs an obituary on Myrtle Shifflett, the Batesville Casket company drives into the back of Anderson's Funeral Home and remains parked there the exact amount of time it would take to unload a big delivery, right around 15 minutes. That night, the lights in the upstairs front room are on later than usual, and Johnny Anderson's Ford Explorer looms in the cul-de-sac long after midnight. The next day, the parking lot fills up with cars that seem to fit the person who has died. For Myrtle's, there were quite a few Cadillac Sevilles, all spanking clean. For the younger generation, there are often jacked up Mustangs and glistening motorcycles.

Here in the south, they call these pre-funeral gatherings family night. This was a new one to me, for sure. Sounds a bit as if we might be playing games and eating popcorn. Well, that is most certainly not the case. You are there to view the body of the deceased and to pay your respects to the next of kin. Here's what happened the first –and only–time I attended a family night.

Now that I've signed the guestbook, there's no way out. I'm ninth in line waiting to view my former neighbor, Betsy's, body arranged dutifully in a satin casket, and I'm stunned that she even has on the glasses she always wore. How strange that I've gotten this far in life without once seeing anybody dead. When my father died, they burned him up. The same with my mother except I did open her urn to put in a letter I'd written in case she had any doubts about what kind of job she had done raising us. The woman in front of me worked with Betsy at the census bureau. She's crying hard, and the irony of their shared occupation is what keeps me from doing the same. Betsy hung her laundry on the line with such care most days I wished she'd just leave it there—a prayer flag, unspoiled poultice for all I heard going on in that rented, brown trailer.

the dangers of lying

The first time anyone lied to me I was eight, at a day camp on the grounds of the National Cathedral. Afraid to jump off the diving board like the other kids, I launched from the board's side, my chin striking the pool's edge before my body sloshed into the chlorinated water. When I asked the lifeguard if I was bleeding, he said no. He must have been afraid I'd come unmoored right then and there under his charge. Metallic taste of blood gathering in my mouth, I recognized how a lie rearranges everything—not in a good way, not like in the movies when a love scene takes up disproportionate time. A lie distorts the world in a treacherous way. Think funhouse mirror at the county fair.

When my mother was eight, she had scarlet fever, and doctor who made the house call instructed her to cut her rocking horse's mane. He told her it would grow back. There she is alone in her bedroom after Dr. Marlin has gone home to his dinner of beef bourguignon. She's trying to pat her beloved rocking horse, now tail-less and mane-less, but there's nothing soft anymore. I wish I could reverse time and have an undo on that one. If I could meet that doctor I'd tell him that what he did was shameful, that he rearranged my mother's world. I know this because it is the story she told me to illustrate the perils of lying. What did you learn too early? What do you wish you didn't know?

My mother taught me life lessons by either telling a story or reciting a motto. Whenever I felt overwhelmed about my schoolwork, Mommy would recite one of her favorite sayings: finish in style. If I wanted to drop out of a sport or ballet class, she would not let me. She would say, *finish in style*. And that was that. She had explained that people will remember your dropping out, that is how your reputation will be left. More importantly, she said, it would make me feel disappointed in myself, something I would deeply regret. She would frequently recite her high school motto: festina lente which means make haste slowly. And it took me many years to understand that oxymoron, but when I did it made perfect sense. When you have a full sink of dishes, wash one dish at a time, one by one by one, until you have them all squeaky clean. *Make haste slowly*. That's a lesson I have relied upon many a time.

In school, we learned cursive by tracing letters that were dotted. We were to fill in the glorious capital "F" or swooping "L". We spent hours on end doing this. Mrs. Adams would sit at the front of the room, smoking a cigarette and talking on the phone while we traced letters. Once we'd finished, we stood in line at her desk and waited while she circled which of our L's was the best one, which of our a's the cleanest. It took great patience, was very quiet, and I loved it. I loved how we were focusing on something so specific and how we were not allowed to talk. And how the authority of the teacher was clear. We never questioned it. We made haste slowly.

suspension of disbelief

Growing up means leaving things behind. It would be a mistake to forget them, but to set them aside opens up a kind of spaciousness. My mother was a staunch—no, she was a strident—agnostic. She could not reconcile all the literature she read, all the mythology she knew, and all the isolation she imposed upon herself with the existence of God. She couldn't let it make sense to her. Plainly said, she couldn't suspend her disbelief. It's not that she would not. She could not.

As a safeguard against this, as a kind of antidote, I keep a running list of proof of God's existence. It is my God Exists List, and I add to it whenever another instance presents itself. A few weeks back, the addition was an Allen wrench. Significance? You may ask. On the steepest hill of my run, as I'm huffing and puffing and hating it all, lo and behold there on the road is an Allen wrench, durable tool, exuding stamina. Plus, providentially, I'd just acquired a bike and needed that very wrench to lower the seat. To my way of thinking that was God's way of saying, *Yup, I'm here. I've got your back.*

A list is something you can add to. You can check things off and feel good about them. But with my God Exists List, I only add. Yesterday it was a heart-shaped puddle on a side street in Philadelphia where I found myself lost during a walk. That heart was a kind of cairn, an indication of a path, a way through, beguiling glimmer of sun in a puddle, sign that I might not be lost after all. I could make it back to the conference center just in time to give my talk. Outside my window at an Airbnb, there is a tree loaded with heart-shaped leaves: God exists.

Here's another: I'm walking to CVS because I hate my new haircut and have devised a plan to pin it up all whimsically with barrette clips. I meander around the store, which is more of a variety store than a drug store or pharmacy, aisles with umbrellas and wine, batteries, and coffee mugs. Once I find the entire row dedicated to hair accessories, and once I land on the pack that might solve my problem, the woman at checkout effusively shares how she loves those clips and how just a couple of months ago, before Mother's Day, they got in a delivery of orchids which used miniature versions of the clips to keep the alarmingly delicate flowers in place. All of this would seem completely insignificant and unworthy of placement on any list were it not for the fact that on my way to this errand I passed a young woman sitting on a bench holding an orchid in her lap, a sight lovely and peculiar enough to take note of. I choose to see this as a kind of calling card from God. Choose to see it as God's way of saying, on that rather ordinary Friday, that the world is not what we expect, that there is much more we must keep our eyes open for. It brings to mind Pierre Teilhard de Chardin's quotation: *We are not physical beings having a spiritual experience. We are spiritual beings having a physical one.*

A few weeks back I'm in Wilmington North Carolina, and I stop at Port City Java to buy coffee and something to eat. They have eggs and cheese, and that's what I land on. The red-headed girl behind the counter, full of zest and positive vibe, asks if I want it on toast, a bagel, or an English muffin. I'm most always—like 99% of the time—a whole wheat toast eater in these instances. But for some reason, I order a muffin. I tote it to my car, buckle in, turn back onto route 40 east, and the very first vehicle that passes me is a Thomas' English muffin truck. You can call this coincidence, but I choose to believe it is something far more resplendent. It offers great hope. I'm becoming more and more convinced that God makes surprise appearances. And it's the most critical job in life to be on the lookout for them.

Recently, I made the decision to expand my requirements for being on the list, to make the parameters a bit larger. Have it be less stringent. People talk about thin places where one feels closer to God, where God's presence engulfs you, where you experience God's peace. Some people feel it at the beach or high on a mountain top. Some travel to monastic ruins or Tintern Abbey to encounter it. But what if we looked actively for thin moments in the places we already are? See, over there, to your right, that shadow? Maybe that's God's way of reaching down to keep you company this very day. I think we all need that reminder. Some days more. Some less. Until you know a thing for sure, you have to rely upon imagination.

Most often I write down any addition to the list on the back of a napkin or a store receipt and then later transfer it to my journal. Here's an example of one: I've parked my car on the side of the road in a private neighborhood, an upscale place that prominently warns you not to trespass. But I love the way the road is smooth and the fact that there are cows in pastures outside some of the larger homes. There are even Belted Galloways who remarkably resemble Oreo cookies, black with a clean white stripe down the center. So that's why I run there—or why I did that day in November. Chugging back up the final hill to my car, I see something on my windshield under the left wiper, something yellow, a ticket or enraged note. I brace myself for the bad news. Instead, wedged under the wiper blade is a flawless sycamore leaf in the shape of a heart: God's calling card for sure.

Another addition came the day after Emma was a first responder for a fatal train accident in the small town where we live. The sights and smells of that day were indelible. The train, carrying GOP members to the Greenbrier for a retreat, hit a trash truck which crossed the tracks at the wrong time. The truck's driver thought the signal was false as that train was chartered, not expected. The accident killed the truck's passenger and injured many on the train. The next morning, when my daughter was catatonic, unable to peel herself from the bed, I looked down at the quilt my friend made Emma for high school graduation. The quilt is a mosaic of her clothes: the blanket she came home from the hospital in, the dress she wore to the first day of school, her first sleepy suit. Well, I looked down, and there was her smocked dress with none other than a train on the smocking. I ask you this: how many little girl's smocked dresses have trains? I had never even noticed it had that specific motif on it before, not even when she wore it in kindergarten.

During one of the hardest poses in yoga, the teacher tells us that God has circled this place where we are right now on a map, that each of us has a spot God has chosen for us. Her voice is smooth, and I believe her unconditionally. She says it again during savashina when I am relieved to hear those words, my body so worn out from the heat and the sweat, I want to just be in that circled place for as long as I possibly can. And what if she's right? What if God does indeed have a map, the kind you stick colored pins in to indicate the places you've traveled? What if God circles the location where each one of us needs to be at particular moments in our lives?

Sometimes when God's exceedingly busy—but still wants to lend us a hand—God shows up briefly, just pops in en route to another house call. That's when I miraculously find my favorite fine point pen wedged between couch cushions. Or the jar of pasta sauce I've been tussling with opens—*kahpop*. Outside Great Valu last week, after a stifling day of meetings and hard decisions, I eyed something flashing on the sidewalk, flashing on and off, on and off, red and white. It was cold and raining and getting dark, but I stooped down to pick up what caught my eye, and it was one of those battery-operated keychains, the kind that says *Dylan* or *Kendra or Live the Dream: Visit Ocean City Maryland*. Well, this keychain flashed *I love you. I love you.* I choose to see it as a gift from God after a harrowing day, a stop by visitation.

Other times God seems to have some free time and resultingly shows up in full force, with a well-stocked tool kit in tow. Just last week I was ushering at church, something I do about once a quarter. It was the Sunday before Lent, known in the Presbyterian church as Transfiguration Sunday, during which Peter, James, and John go with Jesus to the top of the holy mountain and watch as Jesus transforms into dazzling brightness. Pretty cool, actually. Well, it's also a time to acknowledge all who are in the healing arts as a way of remembering all that Jesus did for the world. Well, as I'm handing out bulletins to people as they come in the door, in walks my oncologist who, to my knowledge, does not attend church. He certainly does not attend this church. What he said was that he was there because his daughter was going to Sunday School with a friend. What are the odds of that? Healing Sunday, and my oncologist is in the pews. I still can't fully believe it.

When you can't sum everything up, when it's all somehow too much, it can help to remember the pinhole camera you made in elementary school. Through its imperfect aperture, you were able to see better than you had in a long time. It can be a reminder that the handmade, the quirky, and the slightly disheveled often surpass what is manufactured and refined. Which makes me remember those balsa wood gliders, the kind you assembled yourself, the kind that were in a dollar bin at the toy store. Well, those could cover some actual distance. They always impressed me. You get the picture. Sometimes if we let our expectations shrink, we can be delighted and amazed by what is already around us. God being there all the time.

people you never meet all the way

The guy on the stationary bike next to me at the gym is reading the obituaries. Yes, he is. He has the paper perched on the handlebars as he pumps his legs. As you might suspect, this sight is so astounding I choose the wrong workout setting on my own machine. I punch the button that says I'm 32, not 52, and find myself out of breath mighty fast. So, what if my gym neighbor, as he's biking to nowhere, reads about someone he knows? What if he learns that his high school sweetheart was murdered last Tuesday? Or that his ex-boss had a heart attack? It's a risky pastime, reading the obituaries. I want to make him stop, am tempted to tap him gently on the shoulder and tell him about my zinnias, how they are blooming much yellower this year, how they look like the field of sunflowers I once saw in West Virginia. But we never really meet, we are just side by side. Ever think about how often this is the case?

What troubles the cashier at the Quick Mart? What must her heart hide for the hours she rings up our orders? Does she go home from this job to a sink full of plates caked in day-old lasagna? Is she worried about her elderly calico cat, the one she got after her divorce went through? A few weeks back, the cashier and I did meet for real, and it was his doing. I was buying a can of grapefruit juice and paid for it with my debit card because I was out of cash. He looked at me with a grave expression and said that since I was using plastic to

pay, I'd need to pick up two pennies from the green penny holder and close the
pennies tight in the palm of my hand. He instructed me to close my eyes and
repeat the number ten three times: *ten, ten, ten.* Which I did. When I opened
my eyes, he asked me what aluminum cans were made of. I said *tin* thinking
myself so clever because of the ten-tin association. He said, *No, they are made of
aluminum.* He then asked me to open my hand. I did and was met not by the
two pennies I previously had but by a dime, ten cents. I asked him what
happened to the pennies, and his face remained placid. I sincerely do not know
how he pulled that one off, but it was extraordinary.

At the airport, I'm standing near the kiosk where there's a long line of
people trying to get to their final destinations—which, if you think about it,
can throw you for a loop: final destination, that would be the grave. But I
digress. One kiosk-waiting guy looks like a shorter version of Robert DeNiro.
I wonder if he knows this. Everyone keeps saying *I'm just trying to get home.
Don't you see I need to be home.* Everyone seems adrift. People who never interact
in other circumstances are meeting each other, conspiring, making a plan. You
learn a trememdous amount if you listen in when tensions are running high.
The guy who looks like DeNiro's name is Mr. Valletta. He is a salesman for
Dietz & Watson, the cold cut company, says it on his shirt. He's a smoker,
Salem Lights. And I bet he's dying for one, chomping, as he is, madly on his
gum.

Over the intercom, the invisible voice keeps on telling us not to leave our
bags unattended and not to touch other people's belongings. There are a lot of
rules. I get confused when there is an announcement for someone to meet their
party. First of all, why is it called a party? It's clearly not a party: neither part of
that party is where they are meant to be. Robert DeNiro's chewing his gum
even more fiercely than he was before, leaning up against the counter next to
me and looks to be playing a game on his smartphone.

What's good about airport standby is the fact that you might go, and you
might not. The mechanic may figure out what piece is broken, and she may
not. The delayed plane may appear on the tarmac, and it may not. But what's
clear is that you have no control over the situation whatsoever. Implausibly, this
can be a real relief. Don't we spend so much time trying to change things, so
much time wishing we had tried harder? Not in this situation. There's simply
no way to change any thing. I might be here in Saint Louis tonight, or in
Philadelphia, or back home. No real way to know.

I almost wrote the word hospital instead of airport. In many ways, they are
the same. In hospitals and airports, someone other than you is most in control.
Sometimes whole teams and crews have the control. You might go, and you
might not. Few things are any more certain, few as concrete and unchangeable.

Another good thing is there's a lot to write about when stranded like this, so many people trapped and milling about. Sometimes the lady next to you will go get a bag of Doritos and Diet Coke, later leave her bag asking *will you watch this for a moment while I go to the ladies' room*? See how much we have found out: she drank that soda too fast and needs to relieve herself.

After I get back home, I make a trip to Dollar General, and the credit card machine keeps on timing out. The cashier is the most patient person I've ever met. She uses this standstill-in-time to make us friends. At first, she says my choice of purchases—seltzer water, a bath mat, a toilet brush, and a box of Mac and Cheese—reminds her of herself. Well, that is about all I need to connect with someone. Think of what we can talk about now? Some things go in the body, and some come out. Next, she tells me her daughter will be home from the Army for three weeks; they'll go to Williamsburg to look at the streets lit with fires suspended in metal baskets, they'll drink hot cider beside bonfires in an open field.

And she's not neglecting her job. I promise you that. She's punching all manner of buttons trying to get the thing to work. Twice, she's rebooted the register, all the while lifting my spirits not only by what she says but also by how she says it: simultaneously zippy and calm. The line behind me is lengthening, of course, patrons shifting their weight from one foot to the other. She gets on the intercom and calls her manager, calls for backup at the front. There's a backup at the front of the store, and she's calling for backup. How about that?

I look at the cashier's nametag and learn that her name is Sharon. Sharon looks me in the eye and says *just listen to all that is there*. She says it again: *listen to all that is there*. At first, I think *where? All that is where*? Until it dawns on me, she's not talking about the click of heels on the linoleum floor or the perpetual buzz of the fluorescent lights. She's not talking about anything in this store. She's saying something else entirely. To be candid, when the credit card machine reads my chip, and we are done, I feel a pronounced sense of gloom. I wanted to know what else Sharon might say, who else she might become.

If you come across a bear

If you come across a bear, pretend you are a bear, too. That's the safest course of action. And it's top notch wisdom for many an encounter in life. This might bring to mind the saying when in Rome do as the Romans do. At least that's what I thought of. And it's pretty much the same idea. But it's more than fitting in clothing-wise. More than swirling your spaghetti on the spoon rather than slurping it down. If you come across a bear, think like that noble beast. Or, as the radio advised this morning in response to an influx of bears on the Appalachian trail: *if you see a bear make your presence known by clapping your hands or singing a song.*

In the apple grove, I watch russet leaves skitter across the grass as if they are being pulled by an invisible thread. I'm out here in hopes of coming across my bear, thinking it's October so they must be stoking up for the long winter's nap. Kind of like carbo-loading before a marathon. Kind of the opposite. But my bear never comes, just some squirrels overhead shrieking at each other, barking: *yip, yip, yip.* But I'll keep on waiting for at least a little bit longer.

What I hate most about nature shows is how anthropomorphic they are. They say the kangaroos are happy. Well, how can they be so sure of that? Perhaps those marsupials are not one bit happy about having to carry their young in a pouch over the grasslands, through the mulga scrub, and onto the open plains. And I suspect that they highly dislike their groupings being called mobs. How would you feel if they called your party of four a mob? *Matthews mob of four, your table is ready.* Makes it sound like we are known for our involvement in extortion and gambling. So, let's not pretend we know how the kangaroo feels, or the sea otter, for that matter. Sometimes when you leave a thing alone, it can become its best self. No, I correct myself. Almost always when you leave a thing alone, it can become its best self.

But this was not so for my early childhood. Ours was a fighting family, and words were the weapon of choice. We fought with the explicit goal of changing one another. My mother wanted my father to be more present. My father wanted my mother to be more relaxed. My mother wanted me to be less dreamy, less, as she said, scatterbrained. My father wanted Clark not to exhibit symptoms of what we now know is a severe case of ADHD. The way he lost things and broke things and could not focus literally drove my father crazy. At the table, after dinner was over, he'd stay and pick and pick at Clark until one of them got up and left: Clark screaming up to his room or my father to go out, ostensibly back to work, but more likely to see the women with whom he was having an affair.

These were true knock down drag out fights. And I can remember precise details about them: the shape of the watermark on the dining table in front of my place, the tiny cloisonné pillbox in which my mother kept the saccharine tablets for her coffee, the smell of cooked onions, the click click of the dog's toenails on the parqueted floor. But I cannot remember without looking at pictures what we as individuals looked like. It's as if we became other than ourselves during those fights. In the most elemental way, we became the argument. We turned into it. In The Miracle of Restored Sight, Jesus disappears the moment the disciples fight over who sinned. Maybe that should teach us something.

When Mommy and I had a big fight, one of us would end it by inviting the other to start the day over. *Let's begin again. Okay? Let's start the day all over.* It was such a sweet and hopeful way of making up. But we never used idioms. We never said *it's just water over the dam.* She found idioms untrustworthy, suspect. And that particular one I didn't hear until my twenties when all I could picture was a flood-level river moving at full-speed over a damn. I suppose I should look the term up, easy as that is in this day and age given the internet and Wikipedia. But, frankly, I am afraid. Do I really want to know what it means? If I don't look it up, it can remain as it is, a bit of a riddle. And I like that.

But *Out of sight, out of mind* is a phrase my mother used with some regularity. After her doctor told her to limit fats in her diet, she'd move the butter plate to the other end of the table and say *out of sight, out of mind.* If a photograph from the newspaper was distressing—image of a traffic accident or aftermath of a tornado—she'd fold the paper in half: *out of sight, out of mind.* What's poignant about this, looking back on it, is how opposite of the truth this was for her. She really wanted that butter, and she carried with her the horror of the image for a very long time. She internalized things so acutely it must have hurt. She carried anguish around with her the way you might carry a purse or sweater.

In this way, she lived in a state of high alert, ready for the next stab, the next torment. Often, we say out loud what we least believe in hopes that we might be able to convince ourselves of the truth. Just this past week, a friend, who is a hoarder, told me that it's not things that matter in life, but people. She wants to believe that. But, for many a reason, she cannot fully. I am confident that out of sight was rarely out of mind for my mother.

Since we are onto the subject of butter and meals, I'll go ahead and write about childhood meals from the perspective of our dining room table. It's made of cherry wood, is rectangular, and can be expanded by putting in extra leaves if we ever have company. But we don't, so two sections are all we ever use. In the center of the table are three glass mushrooms, handblown, pieces of artwork. They catch the light that comes in through the Venetian blinds, makes them look like they are emanating that light.

The table knows a meal is coming because of the precision my mother uses to set it. It feels a fork, a knife and a spoon flanking a plate or a bowl. When she places the napkin rings and water glasses, the table feels dressed, and this is the best time, before the meal begins. As soon as the people sit down around it, there is unease. Not one of wants to be there. The table hears criticism and disappointment. The table cannot wait for the meal to be done.

survival float

Clark and I were sent away to boarding camp—what people now call sleep-away camp—all summer every summer. I'll say that again: all summer every summer, beginning at the age of seven. I remember being the youngest kid, second grade, and the counselors were utterly bewildered that I was staying through all three sessions, ten weeks. You might think I would be homesick, but I loved the place, spent much of the year waiting for the first week of June to arrive. I went back every single year until I exhausted even their counselor program.

We stayed in screened-in cabins with metal bunk beds and were divided up by Indian tribes: Shawnee, Cherokee, Seneca, Sioux. There was archery and canoeing, tennis, and arts and crafts; and there was horseback riding, my favorite. We swam in the Cacapon River and, on the last night of every session, would float candles down the river, one for each girl who was leaving the next day, the end of a session. Then we stayed up all night tending what we called a friendship fire, oh so careful not to let the fire go out lest our friendships dissolve over the course of the year. That's what the counselors told us, and so we believed them.

After one session ended, there was an entire day before the next one began, and only a handful of campers remained, girls from foreign countries or

California—and me. Because the counselors got a break then, too, the ten or so of us were left under the care of the camp custodian, a man name Asbury who wore overalls and chewed Big Red tobacco resulting in a permanent bump in his right cheek. The girls who were from far away hung out by the pool, but I preferred to stay in the company of Asbury.

His job during that mid-Saturday to mid-Sunday was to mop and shine all the floors in the bunkhouses, and he needed my help doing that. Asbury and I would kneel on the heart pine rubbing Johnson's Paste wax until we brought out a luster, until we brought out the dark resin in the grain, until we made it shine as distinctive as a tabby cat. When we took breaks, I'd stand in the doorway of his shop and sip on a bottle of root beer he'd given me. We said little to each other, but we had an understanding that is the way we both liked it. We both knew that within a few hours, hundreds of new girls would descend upon Camp Rim Rock, footlockers filled with clean clothes from home. And while I would join their ranks, become part of the Cherokees or Sioux, Asbury and I shared a kind of communion. We acknowledged it with a nod or wave when my group walked past him weeding a flower bed or fixing an archery target on Monday afternoon. We both knew that in three weeks we'd be back polishing bunkhouse floors together again.

My last summer as a camper, I earned my life-saving badge, an intriguing phrase if you stop to think of it: life-saving badge. One requirement for this was that we had to tread water fully clothed for a complete hour. And that's called a survival float. Evidently, it's what you would do if you were to ever find yourself stranded out in a vast body of water with no help in sight. The instructor taught us how to disrobe—which is terrifically harder than you would think—in the middle of the wide river with nothing to hold onto. Once we'd managed to wiggle out the jeans we'd been instructed to wear over our swimming suits, we tied knots at the ends of both legs and cinched the top like you would a produce bag. Then we blew air through that cinched top until the wet denim filled up, a cloth balloon. Next, we buttoned up our lumberjack shirts all the way and blew air in between two of the buttons. There we all were, hunchbacks suspended in the murky water. For a full hour.

When it rained for days, we'd crowd in the dining hall, a long, wooden building with screens for windows, so the water from the roof sounded closer like it was inside where we were. As the afternoon wore on, and the counselors came back from smoking cigarettes, they arranged us in lines along the benches, and we made a thunderstorm. The first in line would rub her hands together and the next and the next until a loud shushing filled the room, the soft rain. Then we'd snap our fingers, one and the next and the next, and it sounded exactly like when the heavier rain was coming. And when we clapped our hands, the rain soared forcefully over the mountain. In August, after I'd returned home, my house would feel so empty without all the other children. When I told my mother about the storms, she would nod, and it will be the same as her humming when she drives or whistling behind her teeth when she has heard bad news.

start with your toes

•—————————————►•

There's a talk show I sometimes listen to when I can't sleep, the announcer with such certainty in his voice I can briefly believe all will be okay. We are both up in different places, both of us awake. That's the part I find simultaneously enthralling and strange. It's like I should bring him a cup of tea or we could play scrabble since we're both unable to surrender to the dark.

When I couldn't sleep as a little kid, my father would tell me to start with my toes, each one individually, to invite sleep into the parts of my body: *sleep, come to my heels, my shins, knees, heart, sleep to my elbows, my wrists, my neck, my teeth.* He had a way of making things sound magnificent, even when they weren't. In my flannel nightgown, I'd trundle into what my mother called her sitting room, where she'd be on the paisley love seat, my father across the room in a wing-backed chair. Most nights they'd be fighting about something I could not name. But the moment I came through the doorway, they stopped their argument and completely changed their demeanor. And while I plopped myself down next to Mommy, it was my father who gave me sleep instructions. After he said *teeth,* I'd stand up and carry that image of my very teeth falling asleep with me back to my room. It seemed almost impossible that something so stiff and hard would ever let itself rest. But he said they would, and so I believed him.

Tonight, lying awake, I can't stop thinking of the way nurses ask how much pain you are in—as if that were something quantifiable. They ask you to rate it, the way you would a movie or online purchase. It makes it sound downright ordinary. Rate it: is it a 2 or an 8? I know they are just trying to get to the bottom of things, but it seems a bit like putting a square peg through a round hole. Or like asking your teeth to sleep.

Good sleep is similar to having a great book, and this has to do with more than simply fantasy. Remember Kafka's definition? A book is *an axe for the frozen sea around us.* It opens up new possibilities, expands the parameters of what's there. In that wider realm, you are able to retell a fairy tale and give it the ending you want. Hansel and Gretel grow swifter in their walk, leave fava beans rather than bread crumbs. They open a gluten-free bakery which is wildly popular. They end up providing bread for their stepmother who softens to them and ends up helping out. Sometimes I feel like I've had a visit with God when I sleep. I'll wake, and my forearms are longer as if I've been suspended in a crenelated cocoon.

In yoga, my teacher said *nothing to do but this* as we lay in shavasana, corpse pose. We had all worked terrifically hard for 80 minutes. We'd sweated in a 110-degree room staring at our nearly naked bodies in the mirror-lined walls, so nothing came as a surprise. Nothing she said could astonish me at that point. But I glommed onto those five words: *nothing to do but this, nothing to do but this.* It's comforting. Try it. Nothing to do but this.

In that pose, while I'm doing nothing, I remember how Clark had a pendulum that looked like a swing set: heavy steel balls suspended on two pieces of fishing line. There were seven of them, and the cool thing was that if you pulled one out and let go of it, there began a rhythm that went through all of them. I loved that thing, the steel balls a perfect circle, heavy, dependable, and held up by something translucent, something you couldn't see.

He also had a miniature brass abacus the size of a matchbook. He'd carry it around, fiddle with it, his own worry beads. I'd listen out for the *click-clack* of it as we sat, obligatorily, in the living room before dinner. He gave it to me when he left for college, and I still have it. I bring it to writing workshops as a prompt to inspire. I ask my participants: how many fingers have touched these counting beads? When Clark got a subscription to *Popular Mechanics* for his twelfth birthday, he'd spend long hours upstairs in his room, clicking the pendulum, figuring out how to put things together in the exact way the magazine said. He seemed happy then. *Nothing to do but this.*

the well disguised world

At the farm where Emma works, barn swallows are out hunting, sweeping their bodies over the hayfield. Tomorrow, the farmhand Peter will bail the hay, but for now, it's peeled out in flawless lines, into windrows. What this must look like from a low-flying plane buoys me. It would be enough to make you feel all is right, at least for a moment, with the world.

I know this first hand because when my plane landed late last winter into Charlottesville, I could see round bales rolled out on the frozen ground for cattle to feed on. They looked like gigantic snail paths. The whole thing was as if someone has pressed a button and completely changed the way time works. You know how that can happen when you travel? I'd started before dawn at the Atlanta airport where the man whose job it is to guide the planes as they back out of their parking spots on the tarmac banged two lit flares together like musical instruments. He had a real beat going, a real rhythm—boom bada boom bada boom—as he directed our pilot to navigate the plane. Then after some time in the air, I'm flying low over fields and barns, silos and outbuildings, the plane jouncing about. The sun has come up, and there's hay in perfect rows. What a stunning world.

Before the flight, I'd wandered into the airport chapel. It was nearing 6:00 am, and they were about to hold Mass. As I turned around to slip out, the priest handed me a laminated prayer page and told me to have a seat and talk to Jesus. It was the way he looked at me that made me do it. I took a seat. But I didn't know what I could possibly say to Jesus that would improve his day. Until I remembered that I could maybe tell him about the photographs I'd seen on my trip, photos taken by a class of special-needs eighth graders. They were exquisite, portraits of things we don't take the time to notice, things we pass by. One was of the underside of a Kleenex box, and the child photographer made it look like one of the rare wonders of the world. Another featured the tungsten filament in an incandescent light bulb, so realistic for a split second I could feel the electrical current running through it. So, that's what I told Jesus about while I clutched my laminated page of prayers.

The children had also written sentences about the history of photography on notecards, and those miniature reports housed such lustrous words: depth of field, snapshot, exposure, still, proof, time lapse, enlargement, silver plate, exposure, invisible. I rearranged the children's words in my mind to make an *invisible enlargement, proof of time lapse, depth of field exposed.* Ah, what a well-disguised world we inhabit, miracles hiding in plain sight.

Lincoln was the first president to be photographed. That fact kind of puts things in perspective. I'd long thought we see so much of him because of his iconic looks and his bravery. But it's because the camera had been invented, and now someone could capture him, memorialize him, so to speak. And those early photographs took a mighty long time to take. It was a half-day affair at least. People would get so dressed up, looked terrifically uncomfortable and, if in a group, unhappy with one another, downright pissed off. At least the few daguerreotypes I have of my ancestors strike me that way.

When you develop a photograph yourself in a dark room with stop bath and rapid fixer, the image appears slowly, gradually unfurling the truth. This is how memory works: slow seeing, learning backward what there is to be seen, what we might have missed or never knew we could see.

In all the photographs of my mother, the ones for which she was asked to pose, she looks reliably put out. Except for one. She's sitting on the porch stoop of our house with me on her lap, Clark beside us holding a stuffed Humpty Dumpty, and she radiates pride. I look at it a lot. It feels otherworldly, almost.

We can see the unseeable: a black hole. Astrophysicists rejoiced. And so might we. The Horizon telescope stupendously photographed a black hole in the winter of 2019. Yes, that thing we learned could not be photographed because you can't see the unseeable. It's 50 million light years away, six billion times more massive than our sun with such a strong gravitational pull that if anything passes its threshold, it gets pulled in, sucked in, never to return. We've *seen the unseeable*, three words I can't keep from turning over in my mind. But maybe what's even more remarkable is how scientists figured out the black hole was even there. They believed without seeing. Maybe this has more to do with faith than we thought.

Since we have approached the topic of what is hidden, what is covered up, I'll tell you that some people I know work secretly and on the side for the CIA. At least that's what I think. Take Walt, my brother in law. Walt's as quick as a lark and has the kind of memory that makes you feel sorry for yourself, meaning, he recalls even minute details of what you said or did months, years, even decades later. And his job is for the Masonic Lodge as their Worshipful Master. Now I know the Masons are the real thing, and that George Washington was one, but would that constitute a full-time gig? Plus, why does Walt travel so much? He claims to be checking on Masonic lodges, but I have my doubts. What, precisely, is he checking? How many water glasses they have? If the floors need refinishing? How the roof is holding up? Walt would make the quintessentially perfect spy. He's always taking it all in, is gracious the way his North Carolina roots groomed him to be; he is funny, quick-witted and, as I said, Walt forgets nothing.

Then take my next-door neighbor growing up, Ted Sherburne. He went to M.I.T., and his job was as editor of *Science Weekly*. When he claimed to be traveling to Oslo, Sweden to judge a 7th-grade science fair contest, hazard a guess at what he was really doing? Yup, you got it. He was on a mission. Meeting with the Swedes to dispute the patenting of the modern-day propeller. Like Walt: Mr. Sherburne was the perfect spy. It quickens my heart to think this way. I imagine I'm being let in on a top secret. Someday I'll wink at Walt over the Thanksgiving turkey, and he'll know I know, but we'll never tell another soul.

why i don't shower

Like many people, I've had my doubts about the existence of a higher power, a god. This was definitely the case when my dad died right on the brink of my adolescence. The news of his death came in the form of a phone call, and I was in the shower. During those few minutes that my head was being splashed by warm water, my mother picked up the receiver and heard the fact that my father was now dead. It was a heart attack, a quiet one, in his partner's office in a chair. He was a lawyer, had successfully challenged the Hatch Act in 1979. Because of his tireless work, letter carriers and trash workers enjoyed newfound freedoms for many years. When he died, he was arguing against the removal of oil from fragile shale rock in Colorado. He'd just won his case, was utterly exhausted, and literally had a heart attack right there in his partner's office. His chin had dropped to his chest. At least that's what I was told. It looked like he was taking a cat nap. At least that's what I was told. Maybe they just said it so the news would have the name of an animal in it. But still, I choose to believe it.

That night, I called my best friend to tell her, and she suggested I just think of it all as an extended business trip. My father traveled all the time for work, after all, so this trip could just be longer. And that did work to help me maneuver the weeks and months ahead. *He's on a trip*, I would tell myself. He's just out west helping the environment. Still, I can count on two hands the number of times I've taken a shower since then. I bathe. That way, I can hear if something happens. Or if it doesn't.

Things that are uncountable: fish in the sea, leaves on the forest floor, raindrops, thoughts, sand on the beach, the times I've tried to remember what my father looks like but can't. Today, when I close my eyes, I see feathers. Not a specific kind, no recognizable species of bird, no hawk or blue jay, just feathers. And they look so invitingly soft. And this makes me think that if you take the "e" out of *feathers* you get *fathers*. Feather becomes father. Not entirely sure what to make of that. When I was in elementary school, and we sang *My Country, 'Tis of Thee*, I interpreted the line *land where our fathers died* literally. Looking around me, I tried to calculate how many of my classmates' dads were dead and why we were singing this rather lilting song about it in school. It made me wary, frightened, that it was an omen, that my father would die in this land, and I was singing as a way to prepare for it. And it ended up being true.

After that phone call, long after, months after, years after, all the way to today, I get this irrepressible feeling that I need to disappear. And so, I am now going to demonstrate how to do that. You begin by closing your eyes and imagining where you most want to be. Do you thirst for the beach or the mountains? A canyon, a dell, a river stream? Once you've landed on the right spot, envision Van Gogh's Room in Arles, how everything is off-kilter. This will prepare you to make the next move, which is staying as still as you possibly can. Stay as still as you can in your chosen place and focus on your breathing. No one can see you. You are in your place alone.

I suspect many of us dream of being an apparition, ghost-like, able to appear at just the right moment, and then to vanish at the turn of a dime. Feel out of place? Show up too soon for a party? Don't know what to say to the marriage counselor? Well, disappearing would be just the right solution, the best choice. Given the choice of invisibility or flying, I'd choose invisibility. That way, I could be and not be at the same time.

When the technicians set me up for radiation, which is completely fascinating, it took about two hours. And that felt quite a bit like being invisible. There was a diagram of where my cancer had been, a map of sorts, that the technicians projected down on my now breast-less chest. They instructed me not to move, not even a millimeter, while they drew, with a Sharpie marker, the outline of where they were going to aim the radiation. They put mini tattoos, black pinpricks, on each corner of the map, tattoos I still have. Which is odd because I'm not a big fan of body decoration. The three technicians talked about me as if I weren't even there. They moved me as if I weren't conscious, as if I were a rag doll. It felt like hiding, both there and not at the same time. To be honest, it was quite thrilling, akin to successfully eavesdropping.

But being invisible and feeling the need to disappear are vastly different, opposite ends of the spectrum. I felt the need to disappear a great deal the day Emma got her wisdom teeth extracted. I'm sitting out in the waiting room, and the only other person there is a woman who is filing her nails, methodically sweeping the emery board until she has something just about perfect. On the television is a show where people assiduously scour an outdoor flea market in hopes of finding rare wonders. We are both watching it, both our mouths agape, when the nail filer says, *you really have to have an imagination.* Which makes me wonder if she means imagination to be on the show or imagination to be alive, paralyzed, as I am, with fear for what is happening at this very moment to Emma. Today's flea-market-find theme is The Golden Age of Hollywood, all mirrors and gilt and lacquer. Far in the doctor's back room, my daughter's under anesthesia. The flea market contestants' time is running out. The nail filer shifts in her chair looks straight at me and says, *you know, life has no guarantees.*

I felt the urge to disappear searingly a decade after my father's funeral when I found out that my mother had been in attendance. *How could she bear to have been there* is all I could think. She had slipped in after the guests were seated, after the opening hymn. And she could have succeeded in keeping her presence to herself had we not been riding in the car one day when I was in my twenties, and an instrumental version of *Eternal Father, Strong to Save* came on the radio. In the space after the song, before the announcer came on, she nonchalantly said, *I thought that an ill-considered hymn to be sung for your father's funeral. That is a song reserved for those who really served in the Navy, and he was just a signalman and for a mere nine months. Wonder who made that unfortunate decision?* Well, I was completely floored, didn't say anything for a good long time, both of us riding along, the chipping sounds of the radio our only companion.

When I garnered the courage to ask, she said, matter-of-factly, they'd been married for two decades, so it was the right thing to do. That is was the right thing to attend his funeral. How unspeakably painful it must have been for her to see Clark and me sitting up front with his new wife. I still have trouble envisioning her having hurriedly changed out of her housedress and driven the two blocks to The National Cathedral to slip into the back of Saint Joseph's Chapel while I sat up front beside his new wife.

An hour earlier, my uncle had picked up Clark and me in his new smelling Cadillac to go to the funeral, and my mother was still bent over *The Washington Post*, still in her floral house dress, still drinking coffee. When I'd asked her, the night before, what I needed to wear to my father's funeral, she answered, without missing a beat, *something dark, navy or grey*, nothing black as I was still a child. Clearly, she'd thought that one through.

Late summer afternoons, still wet from the neighbor's pool, I'd stand in front of the window air conditioning unit, wrapped up in a towel, the machine's hum a blanket of disguise. It was luscious, everything stopped, just the air conditioner drowning out all I could not understand. I was eight. And I knew, the way children do, that something was wrong in the house. Something had shattered that could not be put back together. I'd pick up clues: the day my mother, sorting whites from darks to do laundry, threw down my father's boxer shorts and said to the air, *goddamit, Tom, they smell like musk. Did you think you could hide this?* Or when, around midnight, I'd get up to use the bathroom, and my mother would still be sitting on her loveseat, her L & M cigarette perched in the square glass ashtray. My father was not home. I could see her sitting alone through the crack I would leave in my bedroom door, the door kept slightly ajar with a rock I painted to look like a dachshund. The spherical shaft of light from her lamp almost reached into my room. In the morning, there would be his coffee warming in the aluminum stove-top percolator, but my father would not have come home at all.

being a pastor's wife

To avoid any confusion, I'll start by saying that I am one. My husband, Albert, is a pastor. He is steadfast and faithful, and warm-hearted. He is loved by his flock, truly so. He is the kind of person who says what he means and means what he says. He is grounded and steadfast. He is unflappable. When something difficult happens, he focuses, becomes more tranquil than ever. If we run into some turbulence, he counters it with great composure. He is the embodiment of grace and expansive calm. I often think about what it would have been like for him to meet my mother. They both were given more than their fair share of restraint. They would have had such deep respect for one another it would have bordered on love, though neither would have outwardly admitted it.

But I should establish that I am utterly abysmal at fitting into roles. I fail at it. In the fifth grade Christmas play, the teachers made me an owl because the stakes were very low for that position. All that was asked of me was to stand on the stage and flap the wings on my costume. And they told me to make my eyes super wide and look stunned, which was fun. But think about it: why in the world would an owl be in the manger? He or she would be out hunting that night. They must have invented that role to give me something to be.

Since I had not grown up in the church, I did not know that being the spouse of the pastor is kind of a role. I had absolutely no idea that some church members expect the person who's married to the pastor to be—to act, to dress, and to participate—in a certain way. And to do particular things according to tradition. Well, I was the kid who managed to get in trouble for being creative with her elementary school uniform. So, you can see how this is going to turn out.

You can imagine my surprise when, on the day of our wedding, at the no kidding wedding reception in the fellowship hall, a woman I've never seen before came up and asked me which women's circle I was planning to join. Would I like to be part of the Monday Bible Study, the Tuesday Prayer Shawl Ministry or Thursday Table Talk? I looked her in the eye and said matter-of-factly that I would not be participating in any of the circles. I said, *none of those, thank you.* And I meant my answer earnestly. I had no interest in being part of a women's circle. Additionally, I did not know what it meant. Circle? Do we all just stand around in a circle from ten until eleven on Thursday mornings? Seems like a waste of time. I see now that the difficulty resided not in intention but in communication. And Sarah and I are now friends.

For the most part, the church people have been sincere and gracious. And I get to bear witness to the occasional noteworthy and quite hilarious mishap. I like my insider's view of church life. Just this past Palm Sunday—or rather the day before—Albert was out of town. Dottie, who does the church flowers, called my phone in an utter panic to say she'd forgotten to order palm fronds and did I have any idea what to do. It was 4:00 in the afternoon and all the florists were closed. I thought for a few minutes and then told her I'd take care of it. I drove to the river where I'd seen a stand of bamboo and picked a bundle of stalks, the kind with plenty of leaves. That Palm Sunday at Olivet Presbyterian Church, children waved and worshipers clutched bamboo to celebrate Christ's arrival into Jerusalem. And those same bamboo stalks, which he had burned after the service, spent the next year alongside my aunt's cremated ashes on the bookshelf in Albert's office. The following Ash Wednesday the repentance ashes were bamboo. That's what parishioners got on their foreheads in the shape of a cross as Albert recited, *remember that you are made of dust and to dust you shall return.* And only he and I who knew that they were not palm fronds.

Last winter I flew that aunt's ashes to Sanibel Florida, a place she adored. She died six years ago but wanted to be buried with her husband, Earle, who was doing a stint as a cadaver at The Brody School of Medicine in North Carolina. I bet he made for an intriguing specimen because he'd lopped off most of his right hand in a snow blower during a harsh Colorado winter when he was in his fifties. Plus, he'd worked in an industrial factory most of his life, so I expect his lungs had some stories to tell.

I'd kept my aunt in her box at Albert's church because she was a steadfast churchgoer, a Presbyterian, and so I thought she'd feel at peace there. At airport security, they held her box suspiciously all the while telling me they were sorry for my loss. Then they went after that box with tiny squares of tissue they'd dipped in an assortment of liquids. This whole enterprise took over ten minutes and was surreal. Now that's a word I can abide by, that's a word that makes sense to me. Surreal: super real, real on steroids.

I've taken up the habit of writing poems on pew envelopes during Albert's sermons. I'll pilfer parts of what he says and then add in observations of my own and make something new, most often a poem. When he preaches, I'm on the lookout for words or phrases I can borrow. This past Sunday, Easter, he said that Jesus was on the loose in the world. I relish that thought. On the loose, here among us, eating Cheetos or mopping the kitchen floor. On the loose: right next to you in the mammography waiting room. On the loose: hanging out, eager to lend a hand when needed.

One Sunday a month, Albert brings home leftover communion bread. The woman who bakes it, Daphne, must spend the better part of her Saturday perfecting these flawless loaves. In the early service, the congregation eats Daphne's sourdough bread which Albert has broken with his strong hands reciting, *Christ's body, broken for you.* At the latter two services, there's Wonder bread—yes indeed—cut by Fay Warner into perfect miniature squares. It's brighter than bright, radiant, and so good it melts in your mouth. After the leftovers get stale, I feed them, crumb by crumb, to the birds who come to our window. I sing *bye bye birdie* as a titmouse flies off with a chunk of consecrated Wonder bread in her beak.

beyond a reasonable doubt

Now that's a phrase fraught with confusion. It's what you're told as a juror. Roughly translated it means you better be darn sure you are right and missing nothing. Tall order if you ask me. So much terminology is hard to understand. It's topsy-turvy. It wreaks havoc on the mind. Another example: significant others. Has that phrase ever tripped you up? I've got a husband and a daughter and a son and a dog, and they are all significant to me. I've got two stepchildren and their spouses. I've got dear friends, Cassandra and Lisa and Mary and Claire and Jenny and Jill and Louisa. I've got a brother and a whole slew of in-laws. And all of them are significant to me. And all of them are other than me. They are significant others. So, at the doctor's office, what to write when they ask this? There's not enough room to list them all on the form. And if invited to a black-tie event, can I bring everyone? Can I bring my dog, Linus?

We humans seem to be at a loss for words to articulate what matters most. Children know this instinctively. I suspect it's the reason they want to hear stories over and over and over. The same story on the same night many times, front to back. It must be reassuring to find out the story ends the same way every single time. And that the characters stay the same. You still wish the moon good night. And that room is always great and green. Max always makes an appearance in his wolf costume, and becomes king of the wild things. At the end, there's always a hot dinner waiting for him. Ah, yes. It makes me think of a child psychiatrist who was recently interviewed over the radio. The segment was about why childhood can be so difficult, and the doctor said that babies live their lives in much the same way famous people do. Those around you feed you and take you places. They applaud your every move. You are often the center of attention. Everyone wants a photo of you. Then, bang, you find yourself at four or five, going to school, and you have to blend in with everyone else who also was treated like royalty for their lives up to this point. It's shocking, really.

Recently I stumbled upon *The Dictionary of Obscure Sorrows*, a compilation of made-up words for emotions that do not yet have a name. Maybe in a few years, they'll enter the general lexicon, but for now, they reside in this book which lists mysterious, dim feelings. And that dictionary fabulously seems to resolve, at least for me, quite a lot. One word I found is onism, which means the exasperation of being only one person, in one discreet body, in one place at one time. The example they give is standing before the departures screen at the airport and not being able to go to either New York or Tokyo. You are booked for the windy city, for Chicago. Haven't we all felt onism on more than one occasion?

I would like to invent a word for how my mother must have felt when she was told her son could not read, my mother for whom books were more vital than people. What decided gloom would have swept over her when Clark's second-grade teacher called her in for a conference to tell her that he was not reading. My mother would have abruptly refuted Mrs. Stutt in a reasonable way and told the teacher that of course her son could read, that just last night he read her the entire book *Make Way for Ducklings*.

But when Mrs. Stutt called my brother into that conference, and like a child on show, asked him to read it, starting at page four, Clark rattled off pages one through three then began, as told, "reading" from page four. He had memorized his books. He could not read. He had committed to memory every single book he was asked to read. He was severely dyslexic at a time when few knew what that meant. So, actually, the right word might just be onism: my mother was now destined to navigate the waters of parenting a severely dyslexic second grader, to come to terms with that. She had to travel that path all on her own.

the greatest show on earth

I was eight when my father stopped the car, and we watched the circus unload in our nation's capital. They had just crossed over the Susquehanna on a trestle bridge: clack clack of wheels waking the tigress in her berth, the elephant would have braced himself, splayed four legs stolidly. And one by one, the animals descended. We saw the ostrich sashay down steel ramps into the city streets, witnessed the giraffe bending her neck to fit through the door. I distinctly remember being awestruck, knowing that I'd seen something I could not talk about—at least not casually. This feeling was replicated three decades later when the oncologist put up the slide show of my mammogram, and I saw how the calcifications in my breast had formed a tight cluster, had organized themselves. When I saw the look on his face had grown stern, I had no questions, only the clear sense that I, once again, would never be the same.

Miraculously, I'm alive fourteen years after being diagnosed with stage three breast cancer. I've had a radical double mastectomy, eight rounds of chemo, and a month of radiation. Yet, still, I can't find an accurate label for myself. Survivor? No way. That means that Lily and Serena are whatever the opposite of survivor would be. Losers? Perishers? Giver-up-ers? Not. A. Chance. They were far, far more heroic than me. And I loathe the war terminology: battling cancer. How wrong does that sound once you take the time to think it through? Battling. That implies combat, maybe a crusade, perhaps a skirmish. That is not at all right. But I still cannot proclaim that I have an answer. I don't have the right words. But Emma did.

The day I lost my hair was a windy Friday in January. Emma and Garland got off the bus in the afternoon before I had time to regroup after it fell out pretty much all at once in sizeable clumps. So, when the two of them walked in the door, there I stood looking like a plucked chicken. My hair had been a big part of my appearance, so it was quite a shock until you got used to it.

The biggest wall in our kitchen was floor to ceiling chalkboard paint. After Emma saw me, she threw down her backpack, uttered not a word, and marched herself outside into the cold. There, she took off most of her clothes and stood stock still. She stood still for over a minute in the afternoon winter air. When she came back inside, she fiercely grabbed a hunk of chalk and wrote this question on the wall. *Why is it when you stand outside very still without any clothes on you can't feel the world moving?*

It took me a while and some rifling through Emma's backpack to figure out what she meant by that question. But it all came together when I saw her homework assignment was to draw out the earth's rotation. That day, her teacher must have told the children the earth moves. Well, if that's not astonishing enough news, when she gets off the bus, she can barely recognize her mother. So, she goes outside to see if she can at least trust her teacher. She walks on the back deck, disrobes, and waits to feel the earth's movement. Which, of course, she doesn't. She can't. So why trust anyone? My teacher's wrong, she must have thought, and my mother is not the same anymore.

my own version of the truth

• ◄———————————————►•

I'm not talking *alternative facts*. Not one little bit. Certainly not the kind we hear about over the airwaves of late. But, there's a monolithic difference between stating that something happened and un-snaring why it happened. The first is, of course, factual. The car crashed. The boat sank. But there are a multitude of meanings. Plainly put, the reality of what happened is so much more than the facts.

What I usually won't say, what I tend to not share, is what is closest to my heart. I store it for safekeeping. Like a safety deposit box at the bank where you keep valuables or important documents. I covet, keep to myself, what is unresolved or tumultuous or consequential. And I'm not suggesting this is a good practice for anyone. But it's one I can't seem to abandon. My God Exists List would most definitely go in my safety deposit box. I haven't told anyone about it in conversation. I'm frankly surprised I'm writing it here.

Speaking of the list, here is a new addition: I'm sitting in a waiting room getting ready to be on the radio for a project I run offering writing workshops to women impacted by cancer. It's a high wire kind of moment. I will be on the air any minute, and even the D.J. is revved up, tapping his pencil to some beat he hears in his head, sort of rocking on his stool. I can see him through the big glassed-in studio window.

Then, lo and behold, the ad preceding my segment is for a local real estate firm, Remax of Charlottesville. And the voice announcing it is Serena's mom, Serena who told me of my cancer. Serena, who 14 years ago sat across from me on an undersized chair in the first-grade classroom during back-to-school night, told me I looked astoundingly like her sister. So when I heard her mother on the radio minutes before I was to go on air, I knew that Serena was visiting. Serena, so sweet, was there in that waiting room.

Let me tell the story another way. I found out about my cancer from the mother of the girl who sat across from Emma in kindergarten. You might be thinking that it's beginning to sound like a Tarot card reading, but that wasn't the case at all. Serena, the little girl's mother, a woman I barely knew blurted, out of the blue *you remind me of my sister*. When I asked her to tell me about her sister, she placidly answered, *you don't want to know*. But later that day, at dusk, the phone rang: Serena. Would I like to come over Friday afternoon for a glass of wine? The girls could play in her treehouse that was built in a glorious circle around the oak in her backyard. When she showed me the photograph of her sister, I knew I'd never looked at anyone who looked more like me. She said her sister had had cancer. And then, looking not at me but through me, she said she thought I also had cancer, breast cancer, and that I should get it checked out.

The next day I went to my family practitioner and told him I needed to have a mammogram. I said it casually, the way you might ask for a flu shot or a prescription refill. When he hesitated saying I was not yet forty, I told him about Serena. And he listened. He really listened. He scheduled me the next day for an appointment with the mobile mammography unit. And it found something suspicious and sent me for a digital mammogram. Sure enough, the calcifications in my breast had formed a cluster, were far too organized for anyone's liking.

why humpty dumpty fell

Three girls were jumping double dutch on the blacktop below him, and he looked down because even their voices sounded nimble. This made him remember the way his mother sang him to sleep at night, each star in the sky framed in a hexagon from their wire coop. He fell because, like all of us, he wanted to know if someone would care enough to try to put him back together again.

Sometimes I feel like him. Like the cancer proved that people really do care when it comes down to it. In my case, it took many king's horsemen and many king's men. It took stunning skill and tremendous patience to put me back together again. But they did. And I also feel like the velveteen rabbit that was loved to pieces. The rabbit had parts worn off from love. She was full of nicks and missing pieces. And so am I. Much of me is gone, and new parts have filled in the emptiness.

Some people ask me if I am self-conscious about my mastectomy scars. Others ask if I am proud. What I feel about them is complex. They really are the work of the surgeons who bent over me in a cold operating room for hours under blazing surgical lights with steady hands, passing lancets, securing sutures, firming clamps. Breathing behind masks, they might have talked about an upcoming holiday or the moon or how parking at the hospital had become byzantine. Truth be told, I know little about surgery even though I've been through quite a few. But I do know I am grateful for the artistry of those who stitched me back up so can feel loved to pieces.

I plan to be a cadaver when I die. You have to sign some papers ahead of time to make it official with a hospital or medical school. That's an important step. I'm hoping it might be instructive: this body with its mastectomy scars, its oophorectomy incision, its radiation tattoos, its chemo brain. I'm a teacher now—so why not keep on with the trade after I'm gone. My breast implants are an intriguing shape, and the lines and scars remind me of monograms on an Irish linen sheet. I can even make out a shamrock if I try hard enough.

In art, the vanishing point is where all receding parallel lines appear to converge. In life, it's the moment when something or someone ceases to exist. Which I'd like to have happened for some memories. Try as I might I cannot get certain images to vanish. The cake at my seventh-grade birthday party had plastic circus animals as decoration. But there were twelve kids at the party and only ten circus animals. My father cut up pieces of paper and put dots on ten of them. We drew them and whoever got a dot got to take home an elephant or kangaroo. One girl, Alexandra, went into the bathroom immediately after getting her paper. She told us it had a dot on it, and she showed it to us. But what she'd done was draw her own dot. My father was so furious that not one of us got to keep an animal. I'd like that point to vanish.

I'm holding workshops for women who have or have had cancer. Or at least I thought that's who'd attend. But others have come, and how can I turn them away? There's a woman in her early thirties who can't quite explain how she found the group or what her illness is, but she is a remarkable writer and so fragile in her frame, a bird. I love her voice. Another woman lost her autistic daughter to cancer. For the 19 months her daughter was inpatient at the hospital, this woman, Pam, sang for her Billy Holiday songs and showed her pictures of rare birds. She decorated her room according to the season, even down to the less popular holidays like St. Patrick's. Her daughter could no longer talk, and Pam, in her writing, is cataloging all the things she imagined her daughter would have said had she the ability to speak.

I give the women assignments: to write about their childhood bedrooms, to describe an underwater creature of their choosing. Sometimes I ask them to tell a story flip-flopping the details, making it winter when, in truth, it was summer, breakfast when the argument happened over dinner. And each week I walk away changed. How could you not be? They are brave to come and open up their histories to complete strangers. They cry, and so do I. It's amazing, really.

When someone casually mentions cancer—like today at the barbecue—
mentions it like you would a new recipe or a blockbuster movie, something
shines in the dark woods, wakes me up and I'm on high alert, antennae
calibrating. At first, I can't be sure what I'll do or say. The conclusion I've come
to is I have two options: I can pretend to have no familiarity with the disease
whatsoever, or I can feign getting bit by a horsefly and walk away to swat at the
open air. And I'm not afraid to admit I've done both more than once.
Distortion, in geography, means if you take the earth and make it flat, parts get
left out. The poles get enlarged, making Europe and the United States seem
larger than they really are. If you take something like fear of recurrence and try
to lay it out flat, the feeling becomes distorted. It can't be made flat, cannot be
that trite or antiseptic. So, the best course of action is to step away when the
situation steers it to be so. Here's an example, in poem form, of what I mean:

I Offer to Model for Art Classes

Not for the ten fifty an hour the poster promises
in pay and not because I have delusions of seductive
lines or flawless skin. A lot can be learned from these scars
that were my breasts. But I'm told they cannot use me as
a model, told it would just be too shocking. I hang up
the campus phone, glare at an ad in the day's paper:
pink ribbon key chains, ten fifty plus shipping.

looking at the eclipse through a colander

If I try to think up some unanswerable questions right now, I'm at a loss until I wonder if the word tired has one syllable or two. And suddenly the peculiarity of language mutinously comes on board, and it's tired, tire, wheel, we'll, fool's errand, this trying, tiring me out, this thinking about thinking. Be still, riled mind. *Out, out brief spot.*

But look: that man over there, the one with the baseball cap, he keeps on checking his number even though we all know the DMV's primary intention is to fluster. He and I are the same. We're both seeing stars, both have halos of twittering birds, and it's Loony Toons all over again, birds twirling overhead, words wheeling around.

Mohammad Ali trained in combat boots so he'd feel lighter in the ring. I heard this on the radio the day he died, pictured him sweating and bouncing, shadowboxing in front of a mirror, his skin so slick and luscious there's nothing more to say. He wore more during practice so when the time came he could be less encumbered. And this can apply to the rest of us as well. If we can shed extra burdens, if we can choose to set them aside, maybe we will feel lighter, more nimble, when we are in the ring. When the days shorten, less light, I find myself wishing to transform, somehow, to become the kind of being that flourishes in hibernation and emerges lighter, less weighed down. I think I'd have to set myself aside for a while in order to accomplish what Mohammad Ali did by taking off his boots.

But, in a peculiar way, cancer did just that for me. Once the treatments were over, chemo and radiation checked off the list, once I got my pass to live each day outside the hospital walls, there was a certain euphoria. I felt buoyant. I emerged from that hibernation more alive, seeing magenta, smelling garlic, hearing the song of the wood thrush. While my body was different—some parts had been taken away, and replacement parts had been added to fill the void—my disposition, my very spirit, was lighter, more forgiving. Maybe the man who bolted across the East Lawn, the White House Fence Jumper, didn't feel like he was moving at all. Maybe what he saw was his mother backlit in a doorway so she looked less encumbered, more herself, maybe he understood this as grass blurred beneath him. Maybe he was running away rather than running toward. And he'd almost reached the door when secret service tackled him down. I choose to think he had no malevolent intent whatsoever.

Last summer there was a total solar eclipse, and all the stores sold out of eclipse watching glasses. There were warnings that people were trying to sell knock-off ones which wouldn't protect your eyes all the way. In the days leading up to the eclipse, everything felt like Christmas, like something miraculous was coming and we were going to do our best to witness it. But we needed a bit of protection, which many feel we do from faith. You get too close to it, and you might go blind.

My son and his closest friend, who happens to be my oncologist's son—but that's another story—had planned to go to a golf course that's a throwback from the '70s, the kind that is really about golf and nothing else. It's called Swannanoa Country Club, but there's a long building where you rent a cart and get your scoring card. You can buy a greasy burger that comes with chips and one sweet pickle. The lady behind the counter smokes L & M cigarettes, the kind my mother did. You can buy a Schlitz beer or a diet Coke. You can even start a tab in case you want a second burger later. Or a second beer. And the whole thing is priced as if it were the 1970's with 18-hole green fees and cart rental cost at $12.50.

I set the boys on their way, eclipse glasses stashed in the cart's cup holder and sat on a bench with my book. After not very long, the cashier smoker told me if I wanted to, I could just take a cart for free and meander the course. Pointing it out with a cigarette between her index and middle finger, she told me to be wary of deer who sometimes huddle under pear trees (the place used to be an orchard) munching away. She said they were friendly but might scare me if I came upon one unexpected.

So, I take a cart and roll along the fairways. The sky begins to darken as I drift down a steep hill going towards the third hole. It is like someone has dimmed the lights, that gradual. I set the cart's break, don my paper glasses, and see two moons at once. It's eerie and suddenly so much cooler. It is the slowest change ever. Slow and observable like little else in this life. When Garland and Riley return from their game over an hour later, they tell me that watching the eclipse was the same as watching a golf ball meander into a hole, slow motion. And I agree.

When I reported all this to my students the following week, one told me that she had been to an eclipse-watching party where, at the moment of totality, every one of the 500 in attendance stood in perfect silence. No one moved or clapped or oo-ed or aah-ed. No one shouted in joy. Every single person witnessed it in complete and reverent silence. How fitting a response to something as magnificent. Another student said she looked at the eclipse through a colander. She saw it projected on the ground, each of the holes a tiny moon. Maybe all can be right with this world.

All is right with the world happens to be a phrase my dentist recites as he pushes lidocaine into my jawbone with a gigantic steel needle. Dr. Kayton is a spectacularly energetic man and reminds me of a katydid: at my right one moment, my left the next, looking in my mouth with magnifying glasses the next. I'm supine in a white chair, unable to respond to him one way or another. I'm to lift a finger if the pain becomes intolerable. And he keeps on repeating *all will be well, all will be well, all will be alrigh*t while performing his functions. Lying there I envision an elaborately dressed 18th-century town crier announcing *it's ten of the clock and all is well* or Lady Julian of Norwich brazenly establishing *All shall be well, and all shall be well, and all manner of thing shall be well.*

It is a stunning world. Did you know that a hummingbird's heart beats at 1,000 times a minute? That dragonflies have six legs but can't walk. The earth is struck by lightning over 100 times every second. The bones of a pigeon weigh less than its feathers. And get this: porcupines float in water. Yup, they do. See that little guy over there? He even has a martini glass in his left paw.

dumpster diving

•—————————————▸•

Someone threw a set of encyclopedias in the dumpster at Oxford Court Apartments. It was after the students moved out for the summer, and I saw her do it, saw the Lilly Pulitzer bag she carried, watched as she drove away in a gleaming, white BMW. So, I gave myself permission to go after those heavy books. No one wanted them after all. But I couldn't carry more than five.

What I took were the "A" s. And here's what I learned in the book lettered "am" through "ar". Don't you love how encyclopedias do that? It's quite scandalous, once you take the time to think about it. How do they decide how to segregate things? How do they make those distinctions? How to decide where to stop one volume and begin another? Who are these people anyway?

What I learned: an apostle is a person carrying messages. I envision one on a bike zipping through city streets to ride an elevator up fourteen floors to deliver a decision that will change the recipient's life forever. But I suspect that's not exactly what was meant by it back in the day. Which is going to be an intentional diversion here, so hold onto your hat, but whenever people say that, back in the day, I always wonder which day? What day? The day? Still, we all seem to know what that saying means. It means a long time ago, when things were better and people still opened encyclopedias.

Second fact I learned: a story is proclaimed apocryphal if no one knows whether it is true or false. Okay. Now we are really onto something. It is evening. I imagine a couple going to the movies. She buys popcorn while he waits in line at the kiosk to get tickets. Stop. Is this story true or false? They did not tell anyone where they were going. They never return home. Their bodies are not found. At 2:00 am, the babysitter calls the cops. She wants to rupture even herself. Stop. Is this story true or false? Of course, these examples are more dramatic than what was intended, but still, it's fun. Apocryphal: impossible to distill true from false.

And finally: the word ark once meant sacred box. When I read that, I shook my head in utter disbelief. Ark: a box? But then it dawns on me: Ark of the covenant. That pretty much explains it. And while it's spelled differently, the arc that Noah built was a floating sacred box, box to preserve each and every species. God was the first environmentalist after all.

start at the beginning

Logical to do this, but does it work that way? I tend to think not. I see stories beaded together in a circle, a necklace of stories. I lived in London for a semester in college and still feel a fondness for the city that is disproportionate to the experiences I had. I was there in what academia names the spring semester but is really the dead of winter. My friend and I took over the second floor of a row house owned by a quirky widow who had many a rule: *turn on the hot water heater five minutes before you shower. Close the door of the room you are in and have the heat on for that room exclusively.* We spent much of our semester in the tiny kitchen boiling water on the stove to keep the temperature above 40. Right outside the window, there were the tracks for the Underground or what Londoners call The Tube. At dusk, we could look into the individual cars, and it was possible to read the headlines of *The Guardian.*

Everything in the city was expensive, so we learned to concoct a soup out of apples and potatoes, salt, flour, and water. Saturday nights, we splurged on Indian food, and it was out-of-this-world good. One night I decided, uncharacteristically, to go a midnight movie alone. Having done no research on it and not even knowing who David Lynch was, I scooted out merrily. To summarize: the movie is about a severed ear, a kidnapped child, psychopathic criminals, and sex. To say it is disturbing is a vast understatement. When the movie let out, I climbed the stairs down to the Underground to find the wire accordion gates closed. Down there in the dark amplified the residual feelings of horror brought on by the movie.

There was a woman who lived in our neighborhood, but I only know parts of her story. She had a grocery cart and rather than piling it with her belongings—protected in black bags—she had dozens of cans of cat food. Of course, I felt the pull to follow her one day after having passed her for weeks on end. And lo and behold, she did what you might have expected. She went to Cavendish Park and fed the cats. About seven of them came to her as if they were her very own, as if she owned them. Which I hope she felt she did. After she oh-so-slowly peeled back the lids of five cans, she set them in a perfect semi-circle at her feet, and the cats swarmed around her, some sidling up to brush against her legs, others going straight for the food. You could hear them purring, and even more wondrously, you could hear her humming: pure contentment.

This bright light, this story, comes to me when you ask where I'd like to travel. But I don't want to go back to northeast London. In fact, London doesn't even make my top ten list these days. But I think we carry around with us this necklace of lights and different lights flicker more brightly without any real logic to it.

Not long ago, 50 baboons escaped from their cages at the Paris Zoo. They held a meeting—the paper said they *congregated*—around a fake rock that is the centerpiece of the zoo. Just picture them, this troupe of baboons together in all their glory. I choose to think of it as not extraordinary. They are smart, after all. And social. They just wanted to be together by the big rock. But it's good news for them. And since good news does not sell, we heard very little about it. But it sure makes me want to go there and meet them, those baboons. And that story is a kind of circle. It has no real beginning because they might have done it before. And it has no end because they will surely figure a way to do it again.

A Brief History of Longing is what I once considered entitling my first novel. Until I recognized that it would be completely misleading. How in the world could there be anything brief about longing? Even the word implies something sustained, something prolonged. The word comes from the German and used to mean *to dwell in thought, to yearn*. I like that: to dwell in thought, as if it were a house, a place to be. And if you take the time to think about it, it is. Longing strikes me like that. It is a dwelling place, something you occupy. And I own my longing. You own yours. That's that. No two ways about it, as my mother used to say. And she is the first to pop into my mind when I say longing. Because she was an expert at remaining distant while alive, now that she's twenty years dead, I want her more than ever. And the closest thing I have to her are books, which are, after all, true companions, some kinder than others. Remember a few years back when the novel titles became unbearable? The memory keeper had a daughter, the zookeeper a wife, the time traveler—he was even able to sustain a successful long-distance relationship. How did she pull that one off?

The snow is like living inside a pearl, my friend Claire says when I call in need of cheering up. The snow is like living inside a pearl. That's alabaster, gorgeous, a cocoon. I sticky-note reminders of the snow cocoon on pretty much every surface: the refrigerator, the bathroom mirror, even the piece of jagged slate on which I write cheerful notes for Emma and Garland so when they get off the school bus, that strange canister of motion, they'll somehow be restored to their former selves. At the end of most days, they resemble pieces of waterlogged Irish linen. I need to squeeze the burdens out so they'll stay afloat.

In comic books, when nothing of substance happens, entire parcels of time are skipped over until there's another superhero move. If only this were so in real life.

lefties

My affection for left-handed people is immense. On the first day of any class, I scope the room looking for southpaws and secretly nod to myself. I do a mental checklist, April in the second row: left-handed; Jamil in the back, also a leftie. To be honest, it is a prejudice. I expect they will be the stronger students, gifted ones. Think Napoleon, Da Vinci, Babe Ruth, Barack Obama, Charlie Chaplin, Michelangelo, Whoopi Goldberg, James Garfield—the second president to be assassinated after whom my childhood street was named—and my mother.

My mother wrote with a black flair pen and curved her hand, hook-like, so as not to smudge what she had already written. There is certainly a lot to contend with being left-handed. The world favors right-handed people. Notice the way phones are placed on desks in an office? Think of scissors and classroom desks and water fountains and spiral notebooks and stick shift cars. The list goes on. But things have gotten better. When my grandmother first showed preference for her left hand, her parents tied it behind her back until she learned to use the right one. To be left-handed was considered sinister. That's the word in Latin, *sinistra*, meaning sinister.

My mother's handwriting was flawless. After I left home, she'd send bits of opinion, the way someone else might send news. On a postcard of Monet's *The*

Bridge at Argenteuil, she wrote: *Isn't this wonderful-tranquil, the essence of summertime.* She'd cut out the listing of our neighbors' house from *The Washington Post*'s real estate section, proclaiming: *How do you like the ad? A large small house—pool sized garden—fantasy talk! And look at the price!* She wrote her 'e's like a lowercase c with a straight line coming out of the center, a tongue. This was the only letter not in cursive. Once, on a trip to Baltimore, she sent me a postcard, British painting entitled *Ise Biggest.* Her message to me: *A wonderful piece of kitsch. Our lunch was delicious. Talk soon.*

I believe that being left-handed is a gift, sign of creativity. Bill Gates and Leonardo Da Vinci: lefties. During swimming lessons, our left-handed teacher threw coins in the water in the deep end. He did this to get us used to going down down down, to get us used to the moment when it felt a bit desperate, not breathing. It was an almost frenetic feeling like we'd be stuck there without a way to breathe in ever again. It's hard for me to remember every sensation, but I do recall the euphoria in coming back up to the surface and taking that first breath. And looking at the teacher's left hand. He had a lean body and told us to imagine we were water sow bugs.

When that memory came back to me, I had to look up what a water sow bug is only to learn that they are not bugs at all. They are—brace yourself—crustaceans, cousin to the lobster. Say that word and I'm on the pier at Boothbay Harbor, smell of pulled butter and corn on the cob and beer. While they boil your lobsters—put them in a string bag along with the corn and dunk the whole shebang into a huge vat of boiling water—you can walk down on the docks and look into the boats berthed there, hear the squeak of the gunwales bouncing against the rubber bumpers and behold the stacks of lobster traps all covered with barnacles and seaweed. And there are colored buoys, marked as belonging to a particular lobsterman. It's one trade that is still passed down through families. You can't just pop on up to Maine and launch a career as a lobsterman. Your father and his father and his father before them would have had to have done this. One of the remaining, rare wonders of the world.

special assistance needed at the fashion plumbing desk

That's what I hear over the intercom at Lowe's where I've come to purchase a grill and some shop vac bags. I cringe to even imagine my mother hearing the phrase *fashion plumbing desk*. It would have unmoored her. She would have said, *how farcical, how absurd*. After all, what is fashion plumbing? I know you can get super expensive fixtures, those made to look like you are in a French patisserie's washroom, but still—fashion plumbing? And that glommed together with the rather somber phrase special assistance. I would like to reserve that for blind or disabled individuals, for someone needing a wheelchair or help negotiating an airport.

Also at Lowe's is an entire aisle with a blue sign that reads *As Seen On TV*. We can turn on a light with the clap of a hand. And fold up the magnified mirror we use to inspect our chin hairs. There's even a Dust Daddy which gets into the tiniest cracks and crevices—spooky on many levels. I'm in this big box store because I've gotten lost after visiting my friend's father in a nursing home. Piled against all four walls of his tiny apartment are boxes meticulously stacked, and it makes me wonder if even regret can be contained. The moment I walked into the unit, he looked at me tenderly and told me to go find Jesus in the bedroom.

I didn't know what to do after that, after I picked up the figurine and turned it over and over in my hand. How long should I stay standing next to his bedside commode? My friend was out of town and asked if I could pop in on her dad to make sure he was doing okay. So, I counted, slowly, to ten, and then twenty, before I walked back to where he sat alert in his armchair and told me with great resolve that at his church the organist practices every Friday morning, that the stained-glass windows need re-leading, and that these boxes piled against the wall are *filled with joy and hope amid sorrow.* Needless to say, that was a spectacular visit, well worth any awkwardness.

This reminds me of the fact that once Albert wore two ties. It was during a peace rally opposing the first Gulf War. Walking from his car to the auditorium, he thought he had on no tie. He couldn't see it dangling from his shirt. So, he went back to his car and got the tie that he stashed in the passenger door pocket just in case. He put it on. When the opening speaker bowed his head for the prayer, he began *Let us give thanks for the fact that pastor Albert is wearing two ties.* One was hanging down his back.

book mending

My mother was an expert at it. Each Friday, she volunteered at my elementary school doing just that. She would descend upon the little library, scope out what books seemed to be on their last leg and go at it with glue and binding tape—or, for hardbacks, a needle and thread. There she is bent raptly over a copy of *The Old Man and the Sea*, gluing the cover back on. In her mind the plot unravels, those eighty-four days of fishing in Santiago returning empty-handed.

She found company in the physical presence of those wounded books as much as in the stories they housed. She loved their smell. She imagined how many hands had held them. Also, without a doubt, she would have passed judgment. If someone had dog-eared a page, she most certainly would have felt a sting in her heart for such ill care. She would sometimes say *tut-tut*, clicking her tongue. One time I even heard her let out a gasp. If there were marginalia, she would take a rubber eraser and go to work on it the way she might to get chocolate off a toddler's face. I like to think that my mother cured books each Friday afternoon from 1:00 to 3:00. Afterward, she drove me home, and we'd stop for ice cream at 7-11. Looking straight ahead in the car she would summarize the plot of the books she'd fixed that day, advising me on which ones were worth my reading, and which ones I should pass over.

Fridays, when the dismissal bell rang, rather than getting in the bus line,

I'd walk myself to the library where she would be pressing binder tape onto the spine edge of *Concepts in Science: Sixth Edition*. I remember her showing me how a book's pages fold together in a group called a signature. I remember her showing me how to use waxed thread to resew these signatures before putting the binding back on. It was like I was with an entirely different person, someone happy, someone doing fulfilling work under the buzzing fluorescent lights of my elementary school library.

The day my mother was given our Latin textbook, wonderfully entitled *Libellus*, she stayed longer than usual. It was written by the Latin teacher, Imogen Rose, and illustrated by her students. And while it did cover all the necessary elements of Latin, all the declensions and cases and gender endings, it was a tale about a girl, Julia, with her sordida tunica—dirty tunic—and her ferrum—her sword. Julia fought bravely. And so did my mother, I thought.

In elementary school, in addition to kickball and dodge ball for gym, we took a class called movement. Mrs. Adams had a tambourine, and she'd hit it once, signaling us to skip or hop or sashay in one direction around the green flecked linoleum gym. Then she'd hit the instrument a second time, and this was our call to lie down on our backs and be as still as we possibly could. And we remained that way for well over a minute. I remember hearing my own heartbeat for the first time in my life. My palms turned upwards to the acoustic ceiling tiles, I could hear it, thump thump, thump thump. How strange it was to be aware of what made me be alive.

Since we're back to the subject of school, let me tell you about Mrs. Lindsten. Bea Lindsten was tall and commanding and apparently had one set of clothes. I remember her wearing the same cabled grey cardigan sweater with teeny knit buttons every single day. And she wore a navy blue wool pleated skirt every single day. And argyle socks and penny loafers, every day. She was head of the elementary school, which made her in charge of our weekly assemblies. Each Monday morning, we would file in an orderly line into the gymnasium and sit cross-legged on the floor according to grade, with the first graders in the first row. The sixth graders got to sit on chairs in the back. And the faculty stood. In front of us, Mrs. Lindsten informed us that since it was Monday, we had a new chance to be our very best selves. She said, *Good morning children. Since today is Monday, you get a new chance to be a new you, the you that you want to be, kind and courageous and honest.* She'd chew on the arm of her reading glasses that hung from a string around her neck and say those words so persuasively they soaked in, a kind of osmosis.

Then she'd read us part of a book, *Where the Red Fern Grows* or *The Giving Tree*, which I consider to be a perilous book. But we would listen enraptured, sitting on the cold floor Monday after Monday after Monday. Sometimes we had a guest, an author or politician, someone important who had little influence on us. But to the arachnologist we gave our undivided attention. When he whipped out a tarantula, holding it in the palm of his hand and telling us how their diet consisted of snakes and frogs and bats, well, he had us hooked. After the visitor, we'd close with The Lord's Prayer and be on our way to class, striving, at least for a little while on that first day of the week, to be our best selves.

I've taken to reading picture books again. Many are full of a kind of wisdom you have to dig real deep to find in adult novels. My suspicion is that the combination of art with fewer words allows the message to enter more transparently, unbidden. Take *Where the Wild Things Are*. While the language is wondrous and brawny, it's the combination of them with the complex monsters that make the tale mesmerizing. I particularly love the way Max seems unfazed, most of the time, by the fact that these beasts have taken up residence in his room. The book's messages—don't judge by appearances and your parents are always there for you—are presented skillfully with both image and word. That way, it's not too much to take in all at once.

Things I tell myself: that my cancer will not come back. That Emma and Garland will have full and happy lives. That the things I've done matter at least to someone. At least a little bit. And I also tell myself that the book mending was a joy to my mother, that it brought her a sense of accomplishment in a world where she so often felt out of place.

let's not resent fire for being hot

A friend told me that in his branch of Buddhism, the core belief centers around how we relate to what has happened in the past. If we can forgive ourselves—and others—for what has gone wrong, we can be purified. We can be cleansed. He illustrated his point by explaining that getting mad at ourselves is like resenting fire for being hot. Now that's a saying that can stick. Who, in their right mind, would resent fire for being hot? It just is. And so are we. And so are our pasts.

I think of this when I remember that for years, Emma wanted me to see what she saw, something she still does. She wanted it so mightily I could see it in her face and in the way she wrung her little hands. She'd say *look, look at how the beetle is crossing the floor*. But what she needed was for me to feel the beetle's scooting as a kind of pilgrimage the way she did. She was almost desperate that I do. Invisibly, she must have been working through some element of cleansing.

Let's not resent fire for being hot. The barred owl perched on the sycamore branch stares me straight in the eye for a full 90 seconds, so I name her Joan after my mother. And I see her on what would have been my mother's 80th birthday. I'm sure the owl is a *she*—but does it matter, really? In the most important ways, my mother was genderless. She wore pants suits before that became a thing. One I remember above all was orange and polyester—I'm not kidding. The buttons were big and white and plastic with four holes.

We talk about buttonholes but never about the holes in buttons. Sometimes there are two, sometimes three or four, sometimes one with a little loop in the back. What exquisite care people would put into their sewing accouterments. Remember those silver, metal needle threaders? They tended to have the profile of a woman stamped on the tinplate handle. I'm given hope from the fact that we can still buy little travel sewing kits at CVS. And they still contain needle threaders.

I did not say this right before: my mother's pantsuit was rust in color, not orange. But it was definitely 100% polyester. It was stiff like she could make herself in the company of others, fold in on herself much like a starched and ironed napkin. Diversion: did you know that you cannot fold a piece of paper— no matter how large it is—in half more than seven times. Try it. Take the funny pages of today's paper and try folding it more than seven times. You can't. Let's not resent fire for being hot.

Funny pages and comic strips: take a moment to think of those. Entire pages—on Sundays a whole section—of the paper dedicated to fun, to frivolity and parody. And it's often still printed in color, so it attracts more attention. I like the fact that you can hide behind a paper, too. It's convenient. Needle threaders and funny pages are on my list of things that give me hope. Oh, and jacks, the game of jacks. The kind made of heavy metal are the best. I love how you throw them down on the ground and then take great care in picking them up one at a time and then two at a time and then three. Onesies, twosies, threesies: it's a demanding game, takes patience and hand-eye coordination.

I cannot remember what shoes my mother would wear in the winter. Of course, I want to say loafers, want to say she wore loafers because they are leather and classic and sensible. She loved sensible things. But that is not what she wore. In summer, she wore sandals. That I remember. Usually, they were white and had an inch wedge heel. You could see the shape of her foot when she took them off. The shape of her foot was indented in the leather insole. Not being able to remember my mother's winter shoes hurts in a way that is lonely. It's like I have lost something. Which I have. I cannot find it anymore.

Eight months after her death, as I am in labor with Emma, my mother paid me a visit. That is the most accurate way to say it. She was wearing the house dress with a pastel geometric design—quite the hideous get-up—and she walked purposefully into the delivery room. She just walked in. And she stood there watching and listening, but she did not say a word. She stayed all the way up until the moment when Emma's head crowned. I was the only one who could see her, but I can assure you she was there.

Six months after that, she appeared again, this time at the dentist's office.

I had Emma in a portable car seat and was making my co-pay when a woman in the waiting room said that my daughter was beautiful. I barely turned to look over my shoulder at her as people so often say that of babies. But then she added, *and that baby has a lot to teach you if you are willing to learn.* Well, that made me look. The woman was wearing a pants suit and an onyx necklace like my mother's, and her hair was cut short and dark brown, exactly like my mother's. She gestured emphatically with her hands the way my mother did, and I knew that she had come for that one moment.

After I got back to the car and clicked Emma's car seat to its base, I clutched the steering wheel, bowed my head and tears fell to my lap. These brief visitations, when she comes as an owl or a waiting room woman, answer a lot of questions for me, but not in a way I can nimbly explain to anyone at all.

I have the sense that my mother loved her childhood or parts of it. She adored her father and her pony, Brownie, who was so smart he walked his front hooves up the two stairs that led to their kitchen and knocked on the door four times. Mommy would come out with a piece of bread that had been burnt in the toaster, or a lemon drop dusted in sugar, with a slice of apple. She was a skilled tree climber and an avid reader. There she is reading while lying on her back on an oriental rug, in good company among the rug's complex patterns.

the hardest question

Who are you? I am not a camel. I am not paper or tin or steel. I am not as small as the miniature figures in my childhood dollhouse, the ones who even had on clothing, felt jackets and dungarees made out of blue jean material. I am not as big as the trees who scrape their voices into the wind. I am not a locomotive. Not a field. I am not ancillary, even though sometimes I wish I could be. But sometimes I wish I were a cow because I've seen how they can rub their sorrow away under a cedar tree and how they group together in the shade. I also admire chickens, the way they chase each other, then stand stock still as if they are in a game of red light, green light.

What animal would you like to be? Maybe that's the hardest question. If I were a dog, I'd wish my name to be Dunstan. Those around me would say it over and over, and it would come to be something simultaneously soothing and delicious. Dunstan, like a kind of pastry, a sweet bread. Dunstan, people would call, and I would come, or I would not, depending upon my mood.

My owner would have grief hidden in his breast pocket. It would be our secret, known to only the two of us. It's not a handkerchief, exactly, but not the opposite of one either. Whenever he finds himself in a pensive state, I lie close to help him hold his thoughts together. Later, at the lake, he teaches me everything he knows about finding sticks and balls, about running full-out to your heart's desire.

When Garland was ten, we had a four-foot-long black water pipe in the yard, the huge accordion kind. It was there to help divert rain away from the house's foundation. One day, he picked up one end and motioned for me to pick up the other. That way we could whisper to each other. Not sure why, but the first thing I asked him was if he had lice (it had been going through his elementary school), and he said: *Mom, that's like asking me if I believe in God which is clearly a question I cannot answer through a pipe.* We kept on talking through the tube, but I refrained from asking him any more questions. I love that memory of talking together through the black drainage pipe in the yard.

Most afternoons after he got home from school, I'd throw hordes of whiffle balls for him in the field out back. In early spring, the grass still yellow and hard on the feet, we'd bundle up and practice with a bucket full of balls. He taught me how to swing without looking all the way, to look just a little bit away so you could hit it straight on. I've kept that lesson with me to this day. Now he's 17 and captain of the varsity baseball team. I love watching him play, takes me right back to when he was a child.

In third grade, Garland wrote a new ending to *Charlotte's Web* for an assignment in school. His version reads, *Charlotte lives a long time and raises her babies. She marries Wilbur, and one of the baby spiders spins the rings. The end.* It was at the height of my cancer treatments, after the third round of chemo, the day after my friends had gathered and cut my once-long hair into a pixie so there' be less to contend with when it did fall out. One friend told me she took a hunk of the hair and put it in her grandfather's favorite maple tree in hopes that a bird would build its nest of it. Garland knew all this, saw it, so his new ending is quite a hopeful thing.

No one has ever seen the eighth-grade science teacher's ankles, Garland told me on his way home from school in the spring of that year. He said it in a reporting kind of voice, factually, so there was no temptation to question him. I just believed him at face value. Still do. But that was years ago. I love the way he said it and how it has stuck with me all these years. I also treasure how, in tenth grade, Emma decided to go to school one day as a double agent. The name she chose was Johann Schmidt. I asked her what she was going to do, what she was going to say when her teacher called roll. She said she would correct her, tell her that she was actually Johann. I asked her what she would do if she got in trouble for being, as the British say, cheeky. She said she wouldn't care, that it would be worth it. So, I told her what happened to me in sixth grade. My teacher was Mr. Van Nuys, and all I remember was that he taught us geography on an honest-to-goodness globe, calling out Tegucigalpa or Berlin and asking us to step to the front of the room and giving us 60 seconds to point to the corresponding location on the blue and green orb he held in his hand. One morning, during roll, when he said, *Charlotte Matthews*, I responded, *that's my name don't wear it out, gotta last me a lifetime.* I spent the remainder of that day in Mrs. Lindsten's office reading. It was such a gentle punishment, and the office smelled like orange peels, so I didn't mind one bit.

Garland's always been straight forward and unembellished in his descriptions. When strangers ask me to describe my son, I tell them that if he ever found himself in jail—which I doubt he ever would—he would answer questions about it by saying, *nice linoleum pattern, but I'm not sure why the milk is in a bag that comes with no straw. How are you meant to drink it?*

One spring afternoon in his sixth-grade year, I noticed a woman at his school with a whistle around her neck, though she was most certainly not one who looked even vaguely like a P.E. teacher. I asked him about her, and he said, *Oh, that's Mrs. Godfried. She's the teacher for the kids who don't want to be in school. She just blows the whistle when they do something they shouldn't. She basically blows it all the time. I feel sorry for those kids.* And here are some of his answers on a 9th grade English quiz that might give a glimpse into his plain sailing way of being in the world.

Question: What characterized the Renaissance?
His answer: *Good art, literature, and philosophy*
Question: What is a soliloquy?
Answer: *One person alone on stage.*
Question: Antonym for humor?
Answer: *Robot*

I love that one because the opposite of humorous is robotic when you take the time to think it through. Yesterday, Garland watched film clips from the '70s in school about nuclear preparedness. He came home aghast. How unimaginative, he reported, that people would even for a split second believe that it might work to hide behind a newspaper or duck in a cellar, hole up there with a week's worth of food in case of a nuclear attack. Of course, we humans frequently trick ourselves. I suspect the other option's just too much to take.

At the public lake, Beaver Creek, local firefighters practice. They schlurp up the water from the reservoir and then shoot it back out onto the lake. The chief firefighter explains to the younger ones how to make the water splay widely so as to cover as much area as possible. He tells them to hold the hose tightly, securely, using upper body strength. What interests me most is how they talk to one other. It's as if they are at a fire, as if they are on scene. But they are acting. I hear the biggest man, the chief, say *over there is a dachshund, which of you is going to get it?* When, in reality there are do dogs in sight. A bit later, he asks, *from what direction is the wind blowing?* After that, *how long do you have?* And that is a question that can be interpreted in many ways. *How long do you have?* How long do any of us have? Hard question.

When I read Kipling's *Just So Stories* to Garland, I remembered my father sitting on the edge of my trundle bed and becoming the elephant's child. I can't remember what he looked like, but I can still hear how he would lift his voice whenever he said the words *all his fine aunts and uncles* because he would take on a deep and thoroughly convincing tenor. And when he read to me of how the camel got his humph, he would say *humph* in a way that I can reproduce for you to this day. He made the kolokolo bird sound like the most impressive beast ever. When I read those stories to Garland, he mouthed along as I read *by the great grey-green banks of the greasy Limpopo River.* It was enough to make you feel all is right with the world.

we sit under shade trees
we did not plant

Recently a friend said this. And I didn't catch its meaning at the get-go. A group of us had rented a cottage, set aside a weekend to write and be silent. And this is what my friend said during one of the non-silent hours. It's a metaphor, of course, but it makes the mind stretch, allows you to think in a spacious way. So much of what we rely upon, so much of what we enjoy, is because of those who came before. How true that is. Earlier that day, as my friend scooted in his slippers around the kitchen, fixing himself a bagel and orange juice, slowly spreading cream cheese the way you might maneuver oil paint on a canvas, I thought about all the rings and bracelets he was wearing and how each one of them must have a story he could share.

He described walking with his young children on the frozen swimming pool that was at the center of their apartment complex. No doubt you've seen those, the apartments all arranged around a central pool. He told us there were layers of frozenness, and the leaves held their colors, some tan, some still russet, some a dark brown. Walking on the frozen pool was one of the rare moments of peace he'd had. He then showed me pictures of his children, Taeho and Samuel and Meliko, suspended on the ice above the leaves.

Around unplanted tree trunks, yellow ribbons wave in the October wind.

The trees are at an angle, slightly askew as if someone blithely came by and knocked them down in one fell swoop but, miraculous as Weebles, they did not fall down. There are hundreds of them. Hundreds of tulip poplars outside this Philadelphia conference center. Next year I'll plop myself down under one of them and make a temporary sanctuary in the city. I'll sit under a shade tree I did not plant. On the way to the conference, the train conductor is named Noody; the tag on his uniform says so. He is gracious and can keep his balance no matter how abruptly the train jerks coming into 30th street. He, like these trees, is a stalwart presence, impressive agility.

I'm thinking of the term *collective noun*. Let's start with what flies: a murder of crows, a charm of finches, a murmuration of starlings, a parliament of owls, an ostentation of peacocks. Next, we'll move onto land dwellers: nest of rabbits, knot of toads, skulk of foxes. Then we have a board of trustees, and a flight of stairs. Odd, wondrous world.

And here are some fascinating facts. The train I'm on has gigantic accordions that play no music. Lettuce will not germinate in warm soil. Florence Nightingale was the lady with the lamp. Horses' teeth keep on growing long into adulthood. Alaska is the only state that can be typed on one row of keys. For a short while, the Titanic was a joyous proposition. My mother read murder mysteries like it was going out of style. To win means someone's going to lose. Penguins are flightless birds. Not everything is made of matter. Not light from a torch or the sound of a police siren. You can neither hold nor taste nor smell them. They are energy, pure, and simple. What is happening right now? Far more than we can say. But the shade trees, they know.

the uncertainty project

See over there? That is the boy whose handprint is pressed into the sidewalk outside the library. He didn't leave any initials, but I saw him do it, and that was over a year ago. After a rain, when the sun comes out, the impression of his little hand sends out bright flecks of light. The writer Brian Doyle described *the shimmer of something in the ordinary muddle.* I love that: shimmer of something.

In the Cancer Infusion Center, Jimmy Budd knows everyone. That's his job as receptionist. But he goes well beyond it. He makes the place seem downright jovial. He is an orchid that surprises you with simultaneous durability and frailty. It makes me want to take him to a laundromat where we can watch clothes be plunged into the darkening water. Later we'll rejoice at how inimitable the shapes become when the oversized drier rounds the towels. Well, that's the shimmer of something in the ordinary muddle. It's also, I suspect, what Van Gogh saw. How else could he make that room in Arles so fantastically off kilter? I suspect he was saying this is what the world is: the uncertainty project.

And so I'll tell you another story that fits into this category. Right before my parents gave up fighting and called it quits, they went on a trip, left us with a sitter who talked on the phone in the front hallway, sat in my mother's chair gallantly switching the black receiver between ears. I kept on trying to get her attention, but it was like she couldn't see me, which maybe was true. I'd become invisible, which at eight is hard to take. When it was time for our parents to return, my brother and I decorated the basement with red and blue and yellow streamers, balloons, a welcome home banner. We even got a cake from Giant. My mother came in the door alone, walked past the whole party setup, and climbed the stairs in silence to her room.

When I think about my parents' divorce, I have a feeling that what my mother dreaded the most was telling her mother. She would practice what she was going to say, almost under her breath, in her sitting room. I could tell from both the cadence and the tone of her voice what she was doing. While I could not hear the exact words, I was able to parse out that she began *I have something difficult I need to share with you.* That was her way of preparing her critical mother. She knew her mother would accuse her, would tell her that she had failed, somehow, as a wife. She would intimate that it was my mother's fault that my father found a younger woman. She would chastise her for it. I know this because of my grandmother's vanity, how she wore shoes a half size too small so as to keep her feet dainty.

I was in eighth grade when our history teacher asked us to map out our ancestry as best we could. This, of course, was long before the rage of ancestry.com, and so it was a bit of a curious assignment for late 1970s. Knowing this would be something my mother could help me with, I asked and she swiftly produced a legal pad and began to spell out the pedigree of the Carson family for the past four generations. She drew lines connecting people. She even told me to instruct my teacher that the correct name for such a chart is pedigree, just like for dogs. None of this surprised me, even a little bit, until she wrote, *Mary Jean* and the date June 5 -June 6 1931. Never before had she spoken of this sister, girl born three years before my mother, girl who lived one day. When I asked her to tell me more, all she would say was that if you ever see a grave that says baby boy or baby girl, that means the infant was stillborn. A named child took at least a few breaths in this world. Later that day, reluctantly, she explained, with a clenched jaw, that her mother cared more about her figure than about the baby's health and that is why her sister died a few minutes after birth. I will never know the truth of what happened. But this explains a lot about my mother's fear of telling her mother she was getting divorced.

Everything has to do with energy. Remember enthalpy and entropy? Our eighth-grade biology teacher was big on that lesson. The day he showed us how much stimulation we can take I remember best. He lined the class up and had each of us stand before him while he waved his hands close to our faces, one by one, asking a litany of questions. *What's your favorite ice cream flavor? Who was Harry Houdini? What is the tallest building in the world?* So, our minds were racing as we were trying to come up with answers, and his hands were waving, and sooner or later each and every one of us backed up and said it was just too much. He showed us first-hand to be careful and caring about our energy.

Horses sleep standing up. Most of the time. At the barn where Emma works, there's a warmblood so massive he cannot lie down in his stall. Benjamin's his name, and he is the gentle giant you would expect him to be. In January his coat gets thick as the velvet drapes behind the elementary school stage. There are times when I want Benjamin to be able to lie down, to rest his tremendous head on the sawdust. Until I remember the skirmish that is a horse getting up. It's like us trying to get up after we've had a fall skating. On the coldest days, I go into Benjamin's stall, close the door and sidle up next to him. His breath is warm and smells of sweet feed: molasses and oats.

Emma's twenty now, and the years have sped like silverfish. I hear parents of teenagers say this all the time, so I'm no different from them. She's running with the rescue squad, knows how to start an IV line, cut a seat belt, get the ambulance to rural roads no cellphone signal would ever reach. She uses a map book that the crew chief keeps up to date. When I think of it, though, not all that much has changed. At three, she advised me on how to get Garland to eat: *Mom, rice cereal. He wants rice cereal. He does not want that.* This is when I was trying out sweet potatoes on him. She said it with such sureness, and she was right.

For as long as people have lived in the community, there's been a need to dispose of what we use. The first landfills popped up around the same time as the first cities. Because of cholera, The Nuisance Removal and Disease Prevention Act of 1846 required organized disposal in London. I love the complexity of that name. The word nuisance used to mean injury or damage. Now it's come to mean what's unwanted, what's in the way. But I love how the British can make even rats and feces sound dignified. Sounds like the workers would be wearing tailcoats and white gloves. Of course, we all know that's not what happened, but, still, I picture it in this way.

Here's another addition to my God Exists List. Yesterday at Great Valu *The Sound of Silence* was playing over their P.A. system. And not two hours before that, I thought of that song and it's opening, *Hello darkness my old friend.* This brings me to the wondrousness of the Crozet Great Valu. It used to be they'd only play music on Sundays, a special treat for the workers, I suspect. And part of me misses that custom. But now there's always music, good music, not your run of the mill canned-in playlist. The next great thing is there's no self-check-out, and every person who works there genuinely seems pumped to be doing what they are doing. What distinguishes it from a Trader Joe's, for instance, is the diversity of clientele and products. They've got an entire aisle for stuff under 2.00. Shopping there I've run into the mayor, my kids' kindergarten teacher, the president of UVA, the man who keeps cattle down the road, the postmistress, and my next-door neighbor, Bill. He had nine boxes of Life cereal in his cart, and ten cans of frozen orange juice. When I asked if he was having a whole slew of kids for an overnight, he explained that no, he just shops this way. Cereal one visit, frozen peas the next, chicken soup the next. He said it keeps him grounded.

This reminds me of a fifth-grade classmate, Bobbi Tilling. She'd moved to Virginia from Hawaii, and her father was a seismologist and gave a presentation on volcanoes which I will never forget. He showed a film he'd taken of a 17-mile high eruption, and it was stunning. But here are the two remarkable facts about Bobbi. Number one: she used the same brown paper lunch bag for an entire month. As the 25th or 26th rolled around, they'd grow translucent at the folds where after lunch each day she emptied it and put it in her backpack. Number two: her mother only went grocery shopping once a month. I can attest to it because I tagged along with them to the naval commissary and witnessed as she filled her cart with cans of condensed milk, frozen fish, hominy grits, and dried fruit. That kind of thing sticks with you. Maybe she did it as a way to bring constancy into her life, something we all crave.

Volcanoes make me remember my uncle, my own uncle Sam, writer for *The National Geographic*, who stood six miles away from the test site in Nevada. He was there working on an article entitled *Nevada Learns to Live with the Atom*. And he risked it all to do this. Which is surprising because just eight years earlier he'd eaten half a bar of Octagon soap to give him heart palpations right before his medical examination for the draft. But maybe he told himself the sunglasses they'd issued him would be enough. Or that the explosion wasn't, somehow, real, that the mushroom cloud people could see from hotel rooms in Las Vegas 70 miles away wasn't going to kill him. It's amazing how we can trick ourselves. Did he back up at the moment of the explosion? Did his ears ring? His stomach churn? Come back from that edge, Uncle Sam. But I'll never know. He died, as you would expect, of cancer and at a young age. Bone marrow cancer, painful and fast.

His office at *The National Geographic* I remember oh so clearly. It was carpeted in red like a church sanctuary, and the walls were covered in felt boards, the kind they stick letters on to announce the day's hymns. And what was spelled out on Uncle Sam's office walls were the next issue's contents: all the forthcoming articles, letters and features. I remember wanting an office like that, wanting to be surrounded by the future spelled out in black and white plastic letters.

Uncle Sam taught me how to make a willow whistle. This is not the same as bridging a sturdy blade of grass between your two thumbs, now parallel to each other and blowing with just the right velocity—though that is a trick I treasure. A willow whistle involves hollowing out a willow wisp, taking all the leaves off, and making a literal whistle. We would do it to summon invisible badgers. It was great.

I accidentally visited very near the Nevada test site. My childhood friend, Jenny, and I were driving cross country. We spent most of that trip eating black beans and rice, drinking an occasional Corona, but we decided to have a go of it in Vegas. We even brought dresses. What I remember were the hordes of food in every casino and the brightness of it all. We parked beside one of those drive-thru wedding places which I found slightly charming with its Styrofoam bells encircling the portico. But we both agreed, quite rapidly, that this was not the place for us. So, we stuffed ourselves back into her hatchback and hit the road, agreeing to find a hotel within an hour and sleep. We'd been up since before dawn, trying to keep from driving in the heat of the desert.

The roads west out of Vegas are straight and shoulder-less, without a pull-off or town in sight for what feels like a hundred miles. It's as if the road builders wanted to keep you trapped in that city, the way the casinos do with their clock-less walls, no way to calculate time, no easy way out. We drove and drove and drove, both of us so tired we took to singing campfire songs. By the end, we were singing *a hundred bottles of beer on the wall* at the top of our lungs, the dark of the desert streaming by. When, at last, we came to a town, there was a bar, the kind you see, really and truly, in old westerns, a saloon, with the door that swings open onto a dusty street. And there was a hotel, or so it said, sign over a trailer that served as the office. We asked for a room and paid what I recall as being quite a bit for it. Our room was in a dingy trailer out back.

When Jenny got into the shower, I looked out the window inches from which was chain link fence with concertina wire round in huge loops over the top. I went to the car for the map, curious as to what that fence was encasing. And yes, the Nevada test site was mere feet from where we were staying; we were right on the edge of it. I yelled to Jenny to turn off the water and get out of the shower, to close her mouth, to not breathe. With her calm, impassive eyes, she asked me why. When I told her, we agreed to go ask at the desk about our safety status. When I rung the bell to call the attendant, a long time passed before she came out. And when I asked her what she could tell us about our proximity to the test site she said she *had no statement to make*, reporter talk. I let Jenny sleep a little while I sat upright on the desk chair and rocked myself to a state of relative calm. It was one of those indelible experiences for sure.

what jesus did as a kid

You can make it up because no one else knows either. There's only one place in Luke that even refers to his younger years. I find this one of the oddest things. Don't we all know that childhoods are crucial, that they make us who we are? So why is so little written about Jesus' early years? It must be so we can imagine it for ourselves, which I find to be quite lovely. Did he feel the tumult of the world even then? I'm envisioning him making, out of straw, a delicate toy boat, a boat that would save people.

Whenever I'm on a ferry, going from the mainland to an island, I envision a movie screen, imagine the whole voyage is being filmed. This can't be true, of course, but there's something about that slow boat, barge-like, monolithic and all of us passengers on it so small in comparison: it just has to be filmed. That's how I see Jesus as a kid, as a child in a movie.

Last spring, one of my students wrote an essay entitled *Jesus and the Jumper Cables*. In it, Jesus walks up to his broken-down Ford to offer aid on the side of a rural road. What's true is that someone did help my student on an icy night in the middle of nowhere, but whenever I read the essay, I imagined it was Jesus lending him a hand in his time of need. I envision my student offering him a bottle of water in exchange. It's a sweet vision. In the most important way, the person who helped my student was Jesus, his charitable act of kindness flowing from the Jesus in all of us.

For reasons I cannot name I think of the confetti at the Macy's Parade that was shredded police reports and social security numbers. All that confidential data now confetti: confidential confetti. All those statistics showering down on onlookers. How surreal it is. I want to say this is the end of this story, but that would be a lie. We can imagine, or look up on the internet, the horrific repercussions of all this. But I'd prefer not to. I'll leave it with those bits of paper meandering through New York's air. It helps me try to un-envision 9/11 and all the particles floating in the air then.

two kinds of time

At least twice each day, my mother would pick up the green telephone receiver and dial 411. Sometimes she held the phone far enough away from her ear that I was able to hear a recorded voice proclaim, *at the tone the time will be 2:24.* My mother would then glance down at her watch, the one she wound every morning, to calibrate her time with the time the phone voice said. It was a soothing moment, all well with the world, all accurate and incontestable. When I claimed her bag of personal belonging after her death, I left the watch's time exactly when it had stopped. I did not wind it. I will give it to Emma the day she leaves home. I keep it in a silver box along with a quotation I ripped out of *The Washington Post: No one can make you feel inferior without your consent.* The wisdom of Eleanor Roosevelt.

A minute is longer than I thought. Try it for yourself. Start the timer on your phone, then close your eyes. Do not count *one Mississippi two Mississippi,* or *one hippopotamus two hippopotamus* or *one one hundred.* Just breathe. Open your eyes when you feel that a minute is up. Beguiling exercise—right? The French philosopher Henri Bergson, the man who wrote *the eye sees only what the mind is prepared to comprehend,* was fascinated with this very topic. Bergson made a clear distinction between pure time and mathematical time. Mathematical time, he taught, is a measurable duration. The clock on the wall, divisible into units or intervals which do not reflect the flow of real time. Pure time is real duration. It's how it feels to wait for your MRI results, for your number at the DMV, to see someone you love step from the tarmac and enter the plane—to go up in the air, over the ocean for five months. Real duration we experience by intuition.

And there are minutes, many of them, I'm mighty glad I missed. The first among these would have to be my mother binding her breasts to stop the milk so she wouldn't have to feed me that way. How it must have hurt, brought on mastitis, been downright painful. She told me she'd done this, which kind of mystifies me because she was most definitely not one to try to put in barbs of hurt. Her breasts were large, so I'm sure this binding was no easy feat. But I can be sure that having me that close to her, that dependent upon her, was just too much. As with her agnosticism, it was not that she would not believe in God, it was that she could not.

I'm equally glad she was not around for me to have to tell her I had cancer. I don't know what it would have done to her or how she would have retreated into herself. But it would have made her sting. I am sure of that. She would have glommed onto the details, the facts, the intricacies of surgery and chemotherapy and radiation. She would have looked up the etymology of the word cancer and told me that it was originally a Latin word that meant crab. Later, when it morphed into Old English, she would say that the word came to mean creeping ulcer. She would have known that the Greeks called cancerous tumors karkinos because the swelling looked like the limbs of a crab. But that is most likely where her comfort would have ended. She couldn't solve the cancer. She could only assemble facts about it.

The day our father backed over our Scottie, Dunstan, who was asleep in the shade behind the back wheel of our station wagon, is also an incident I'm relieved to have missed. All I remember is him walking, shoulders slumped, up the gravel drive of our house, the car still parked at the bottom. I don't remember a fight or a drive to the vet. I don't even remember how I found out. All I can see is the slump of his shoulders in the early evening light, how his form looked like he was carrying the heaviest of burdens, which most certainly must have been true.

My mother loved owls and doves. And shadows in the fall, how the light would expand a tree trunk or roof, making it larger than itself on the ground. I think these presences slowed time down for her, made her feel real time. And she raved about old roads, the ones no longer in use. About once a month we'd go in search of them. We'd get into the car on a Sunday and drive out to the country looking for dips that ran parallel to the road we were on. She'd say how the old road was a less direct path and therefore much more interesting. Sometimes she'd even tap me on the shoulder and exuberantly proclaim, *old road to our left—ah yes.*

She wrote thank you letters as if it were going out of style, which, it turns out, was the case. If a neighbor brought her *Washington Post* up from the sidewalk to her porch, for instance, she'd jot a thank you note on a postcard and then mail it. No joke. Or if a friend of mine took me to the movies. She wrote a draft of the letter first, on a yellow legal pad. Then she'd transcribe it to her monogrammed stationery. Finally, she would read the letter out loud to the air around her. Sometimes, across the hall in my room, I'd hear her: *Dear Dorothy, how kind of you to take Charlotte to the movies yesterday afternoon. She had a lovely time. She said the lunch at Vivace's was out of this world good. I appreciate your kindness very much, as does she. I will be sure to return the favor when another fitting movie comes out in the theaters. In the meantime, I send you well wishes. Sincerely, Joan.* Then she would carefully tuck the letter into its envelope, lick the envelope, affix a stamp and ask me to walk up to the corner mailbox so it would arrive on Tuesday afternoon, the perfect amount of time after a Saturday matinee.

What is your most prized possession? What object would it hurt you to lose? Hard one. I'm thinking a feather or a bird's nest. And what if it went missing—which happens to be quite a riveting phrase. Went missing. It makes it sound as if it grew legs and took off on a journey of its own. My most prized possession is the ability to walk and the capacity to love. And the joy of doing those two together. But if we are confined to objects, to things, then I'll have to pick my engagement ring, cliché as that it. This particular ring was Albert's grandmother's. It was also his first wife's, and that makes it strange, but I like her, and she gave it back to him when they parted ways. That's another moment I'm glad I missed. Envision how the earth heaves up after a rodent has burrowed underground, the very fabric of everything upended. But maybe it was a sort of peace offering. They had lived apart physically for a good long time. So maybe she simply handed it to him. Handed it to him and then went to open her umbrella in the rain. I learned quite early that blame burgeons exponentially, that it spreads out like ink on a pottery wheel. If only blame could extinguish itself, if only we humans would not give it any fuel.

chain link fences

From behind the hexagonal squares of the chain link fence, I watch Emma board an airplane headed to Chicago. I can see her on the tarmac walking with such purpose out to the Delta 727. Next, I spot her face framed in the miniature window of the plane. We planned it this way, figured out how the plane would be parked at our regional airport and how she could get a seat so we could sign language each other until the last possible moment until she taxied away. She's making signals that suggest her seatmate will produce a story, will be someone of interest to us both.

None of this feels lonely or frightening—that is until I can no longer see the plane, until I recognize that my daughter is suspended over the earth in a steel canister. But so long as that plane idles on the runway, revving its engines, there is a kind of placidity. Particularly when it dawns on me that it's the exact same fence, exact brand—Long Fence Company—from behind which I watch Garland play baseball on Saturdays. The airport fence is to keep me out. The baseball one's purpose is to prevent spectators from getting hit by a foul ball. Frost said *good fences make good neighbors*, and he was being both literal and metaphorical at once, having written those lines from his farm in rural Vermont where it's important to keep what is yours in and what is your neighbors' out. But these chain-linked fences serve a different purpose. They are barriers, boundaries, clear dividers.

I've been watching Garland through the diamonds in chain-linked fences for twelve years. He's 17 now, and the games are in the evenings. For the first two innings, there is still daylight, and I can see clearly as he crouches behind home plate, catching. But when the lights come on, he's obscured, he's harder to follow. And I see what a metaphor that is for a child growing into young adulthood. Still, I love watching him, the way he is so agile and so kind to the umpire whom he addresses as blue, a form of respect. He wipes off the ball before handing it to the tall, usually African American, man whose job it is to call this game.

One more fence story: in first grade, I broke my right tibia chasing Henry Greenwalt and Tommy Clyde up a chain link fence. They were perched on the pipe that is the top, walking on it like a balance beam. And I did the same thing, euphoric up above all the other kids playing on the blacktop below. And it was great until recess ended and Henry and Tommy jumped down. A piece of the fence had gotten stuck in an eyelet hole in my Stride Rite sandal, and it held me there as I lay draped upside down, my leg cracked.

listening comes before seeing

That is literally true. In the womb, we hear the sound of our mother's heartbeat. That's why iambic is so instinctual: da-dum, da-dum, da-dum. We heard it for months before we were even born. We also pick up the tenor of our mother's voice and perhaps the voices of our siblings and father, of the family dog, maybe even the dishwasher. But listening comes before seeing once we're here, too. Once we've landed. Listen, we say, listen to what is in my heart. I've always heard my fears long before they took on legs and began to walk: my fear of the children growing up, fear of losing my mother, fear of growing old and seeing it, as I do now, in my own face.

Instead of hanging up the phone when a telemarketer calls trying to sell me life insurance, I set out to make a conversation out of it. I answer his or her initial questions, noting that I'm 53 and of average height and weight. I don't smoke. I exercise regularly, eat a healthy diet. I can almost hear the person on the other end chomping at the bit, sure they have a hot one and are going to score a sale. But when the ball drops, when I tell them I had stage 3 breast cancer, they get really quiet really fast. No one will want to sell me a policy. I'm just too much of a risk. The call always ends abruptly with them proclaming there is nothing they can do. Quite often they sound regretful like they are authentically sorry they made the call in the first place.

Blasé was a word my mother often used, but she didn't mean it. The meaning, of course, is unimpressed or indifferent to something one has seen or witnessed. And this she never was. She could be critical of a person like she was of my first live-in boyfriend who rarely spoke, but that is not the same thing as unimpressed. She was impressed, for sure, just in a negative way.

After college, I moved to Vermont and rigorously fell for a boy who taught math and coached cross-country skiing. Taciturn and strong-jawed, Mike only spoke if you were going to burn the frittata or overflow the sink. Speaking was not how he communicated. He did things. His uncle owned thousands of acres of maple trees, and, come spring, when the sap began to flow during the daytime warmth, we'd walk miles together in silence, the frozen ground crunching under our sorrel boots. All throughout the woods were strung tap-lines we'd follow and check to make sure there were no holes or unattached places. We'd gather the sap into metal buckets and stay up all night boiling off the extra water in the huge vat in the sugar house, a long and humid barn-like structure with an open roof. The smell in there was so sweet and dark, more than caramel.

Even though I knew it wouldn't go well, I had the grand idea that Mike should meet my mother. First off, he couldn't stand being in the city, especially our nation's capital, he made that clear at the get-go. Watching him sit in the velvet armchair in my mother's living room made me want to become a fugitive right then and there. What had I been thinking? How in the world would they have anything to say to each other? Well, they didn't. She asked him about his family, and he answered: *my mom is a nurse. My dad builds houses.* It was quite the teeth pulling scenario.

So why the word blasé? Its etymology points to being wary of overindulgence, something my mother rarely did. The word's sound is, I think, the meaning. That *blah* sound making the mouth open like it has to for *saw* and *gnaw*, for *raw* and *law*. And then that quirky ending with the French e rhyming with egg or leg. She loved sounds and words. The rarer ones were a tincture to her, medicinal and necessary.

chance encounters

Edouard Vuillard was my mother's favorite painter, though she liked Bonnard and Sisley emphatically as well. But I suspect what she preferred about Vuillard was how his subjects, most often sturdy women, blended into the domesticity that surrounded them. A woman sweeping with a large square-headed broom—entitled *Woman Sweeping*—becomes part of the bureau behind her, her dress part of the curtains in the window. When I look at his work, I note how the story of the painting kind of hovers. And there's an abundance of patterns that don't match but don't exactly clash either. One of her favorites was *The Newspaper*, which is housed at The Phillips Collection. More than once she took me to see it—*visit it* is what she would say as if it were a person— and we'd stand side by side in front of that wintertime painting, she in her tweed blazer. I understood that what she wanted was to be in the painting, to be there with the androgynous person hidden behind the paper, to be that composed and serene.

Chance encounters are curious phenomena. Are they chance, or is there something else at play? I think of this looking outside the window where there is not rain, and my longing is not gone—at least not the way my mother is, nothing left of her but a stone in the ground. The bearded man selling lavender at the farmer's market asked if I knew that houseflies hum in the key of F. I told him oysters switch gender many times in their lives. Today is Saturday. The grass is growing. Water keeps on swirling even after it's gone through the drain. Just because you can't see something doesn't mean it isn't there. The girl I saw running away from home had a sheet, a book, and a bag of oranges. It was what she chose to not take with her that I will remember most. It's what my mother did not say that I still wonder about.

In the house in the Virginia countryside we had for a few years before everything fell apart, there was a party line. You'd pick up the phone to call McGruder's Grocery to ascertain if *The Washington Post* had come in yet, and Mrs. Lena Wright, our neighbor, would be talking to her sister about the permanent she'd gotten on Friday, how her hair made her feel like she could reinvent herself, change this life she'd chosen. She said she wished she'd been a lawyer's wife, not a farmer's. What a chance encounter that was, and I learned that if I stayed quiet enough they'd just go on talking, not even know I was listening in. I'd oh-so-carefully lift the receiver off its hook so they would not even hear a click. And as I eavesdropped, I watched out the window where two crows bantered, and spring peonies bloomed.

My father must have dreamed of being a conductor. At stoplights in the car, the symphony on, he'd lift his right index finger as if summoning the cellist. Or he'd lower his palm when the music quieted, He'd draw imaginary "L" s in the air or thrust his palms, closed to open to hold the crescendo. Sometimes he'd take both hands off the wheel to slow down the music, adagio. This most often happened on Saturday afternoons when he'd pick me up from where I'd spent the night with a friend from school. I'd be tired but so happy for this parcel of time with him, and it was like the tiredness became a thing of its own, its own way of being in the world. When I didn't focus on his conducting, my mind would float; I'd remember staying up past midnight and making popcorn with Becky or Lee at their houses where everything was different, where their parents at least seemed happy.

Here is the story of my birth, which I consider to be a happy ending. It's 1966, Washington D.C., and my mother is hauling herself out of a yellow top cab into the February air. The nurse standing beside the wheelchair has a bland face, and the doors to Columbia Hospital for Women open wide. My mother is frightened, accustomed, as she is, to being the one in control. Even as a child she took to beginning with a book's ending so at least she'd know what she was in for. But, in a few minutes, she'll be put to sleep on her back, her feet up in stirrups, so I can be pulled into the light of day.

But the two happiest endings I know of are the births of Emma and Garland. They were moments for which I have no word because there aren't enough ways to emphasize euphoria. I'd labored with Emma much of a full night and was tiring, so Dr. Campbell decided to try Pitocin. This requires a fetal monitor, and so once they hooked me to the IV, they strapped a monitor over my belly to listen for her heart. Because the doc felt he'd better serve me by leaving the room and giving me some time to labor alone, he did just that. The look on this face when he walked back in a minute later was one of utter panic. He glanced beside the bed and plugged in the fetal monitor, explaining to the nurse, a young woman, to never ever do that again. He said a fetal monitor must be plugged in immediately. After that real scare, I began effacing, and Emma was born mid-morning.

Garland was breech presentation, head-first, and Dr. Siva Thiagarajan employed version to flip him. With the bed at an angle, my head facing down, I felt my belly go slack from the antihistamine drug he used. Dr. Thiagarajan took Garland and literally turned him—vwoop—and, in his glorious Indian accent proclaimed, *the baby is now head first and should stay that way*. Garland took his time, real-time, another week, to be born, but when I pushed him into the light of day, I was happier than happy to meet him.

Next to my childhood bed hung Peter Brueghel's painting entitled *The Hunters in the Snow*. It's a wintry scene with hunters and their dogs, and all the characters in the foreground appear downtrodden. It's very gloomy with muted colors. But in the background are two glistening, frozen ponds where what looks to be swarms of people are skating together, having a party, a skating party. And that's a happy ending. It seems to point to the fact that what resides in the background, what is going on out of the limelight, can house ebullience. And I like that thought. Still, how extraordinary that choice of a painting is for a little girl's room. I can envision Mommy loving its complexity and what it said about layers, about what's in the forefront and what's behind, what is obscured but stable.

The second year I lived in Vermont was colder than most, and the Connecticut River froze dependably enough to skate on it. One Sunday afternoon, my friends and I put on our skates and made the ten-mile journey from Putney to Brattleboro on the river. When the ice moaned, we would click our tongues as if warding off any possibility of us breaking through. It was a mixture of fear and calm both at once, which I guess skating is at heart. And that adventure ended safely, a happy ending.

what is closer to the truth

Because we lived right off of Cleveland Avenue, an artery to downtown D.C., the president or vice president would drive by several times a week. The thrill of the motorcade passing was amplified by the fact that you never knew which car Nixon or Ford or Carter or Reagan would be riding in. My mother explained to me that the president was not in the largest or fanciest looking limousine. He was most likely in a less expected vehicle, one that would throw off a possible assassin. The day Gorbachev was in town, she called me at college and said *here he is two hundred feet outside my bedroom window.*

Take everything that's inside your head and put it into the tangible world. That is what I heard songwriter Regina Rector say on the radio, and it stuck with me. So, I'll tell you about my playdate with Amy Carter. She went to school with my next-door neighbors and came over to their house, right across the alley from mine, on a Saturday morning in October of our fourth-grade year. Since Louisa and Anne Popkin let me hang out with them all the time, I was in on this activity as well. Amy Carter arrived in a Jeep, quite normal appearing. But she was accompanied by two bodyguards, secret service agents, dudes in khakis, black polo shirts, and baseball caps. They got out of the Jeep at the exact same time as Amy. Simultaneously, two bigger Jeeps blocked off the alley. They barracked it.

I was an energetic kid, the kind to move in erratic ways, kind of zip around, hither and thither. And I was loud: loud voice, louder laugh, big movement. Well, not 20 minutes into this playdate the taller bodyguard pulled me aside (we were playing on the Popkin's swing set) and told me I could not move that abruptly around the president's daughter. He was kind, and even stooped down to be at my level, but he explained most decidedly that he was trained to react to certain kinds of gestures, and mine fell within the dangerous realm. He said if I kept on, he'd have to take Amy back to the White House. Well, you can be sure I kept it all under wraps for the next few hours. Yes, I did.

In 1975, for the centennial, Woodward & Lothrop department store sponsored a beautify-the-city project. They gave kids paint and a choice of which famous historical Washingtonian we wanted to make the hydrant we'd been assigned resemble. Anne Popkin and I chose L'Enfant because he was, after all, the one who designed the city, designed it after Paris, a city of circles with avenues protruding like filaments on a spider's web. Our rendition of General L'Enfant was pink and yellow, with blue eyes and blue epaulets. He's still there. I checked in January. There's pink L'Enfant on the corner of Garfield and Cleveland Avenue, keeping watch over my childhood neighborhood.

This reminds me that I need to fill in some missing parts about my mother, so you'll get a fuller picture. Ten years before her death, Mommy had written a note and left it for us to find in the top right-hand drawer of her desk. The envelope read *Charlotte and Clark—upon my death*. The letter informed us that she had bought herself a burial plot at Rock Creek Cemetery. It said that she wished to have a plain stone, one that was flat to the ground. She told us that we were both capable people, that we were capable children. And she signed the letter with her customary smile face and two stars as earrings.

Since she'd written that note on the first day of spring ten years before the leukemia overtook her, Clark and I thought it best to follow suit and bury her ashes on that exact day. So, on March 21st, 1998, I drove to Washington and bought a bunch of Sweet William flowers. Hungry, Clark and I stopped at Roy Rogers and got a hamburger and milkshake which we ate in the car. It felt like a pre-funeral reception, something hallowed about it all. As we chewed on our burgers, I wrote her a letter of gratitude for what she had taught us and how she had shown us great respect in all instances. Opening the box of ashes, I slipped in the letter along with a copper heart my friend had made. She would have liked that, the copper, the dependability and color of it. That is as close as I can come to knowing her truth.

The graveside service Clark and I held for her had an unpredictable sweetness to it. It was as if we did not quite know what to do. It was a bit like coming home from the hospital with a newborn and there you are alone with that being and the house echoes, no guidebook for what to do. There we were alone together with what was left of our mother. Rock Creek Cemetary had put up a tent and two chairs at her spot—Section eye, lot 385 site 9—for us. There was even a small piece of astroturf, the size of a throw rug, beside the fresh opening in the earth. We set her box into its hole, then Clark and I divided the Sweet William flowers between us. We arranged them around the box and on the tamped-down earth above. Then we took the seats waiting for us.

But what was there to say to her? What could we possibly voice? If I remember correctly, we each shared something we admired about her, and we both told her we loved her. Then we put dirt over her and agreed that the spot was a good one. There is a tree, an old oak, to provide her shade, and the acorns will give her something to fuss about each fall. She also has a direct view of Military Avenue so she can inspect the cars that leave the city on their way to Maryland. I have faith that she likes it there, in the company of other old Washington families, not far from Julius Garfinckel, founder of the classic Washington department store. There she is a stone's throw away from Gil Grosvenor, past president of the *National Geographic,* and she's not far at all from the writer Henry Adams, a descendant of two presidents. Thinking back, I wish I'd sung her *down in the valley, valley so low, hang your head over, hear the wind blow,* but probably that would have been too much. I have written Section eye, lot 385 site 9 in my address book where I can occasionally look at it when the need arises.

Among the few letters, I received after Mommy's death was one from her college roommate. After Claire Harwood expressed her condolences, she wrote the following: *the great culmination of our years of study together was our trip to Greece, Sicily, and Italy with Professor Rhys Carpenter. We had our hilarious moments on that trip. We discovered that we each talked to ourselves out-loud when we thought no one could hear us. I caught Joan happily chatting with herself on the hill of the Acropolis at Athens. We were supposed to be gazing at the Parthenon at sunset. Some of Joan's soliloquies were accompanied by gestures!*

that one looks like an elephant

Crickets who hover in the broom sedge go undetected until you walk among them and they jump: you and the crickets in the field, quite lovely. In 2010, nine Peruvian miners were trapped, and they made a pact not to share what went on between them before they knew rescuers were above them, were working on how to get them to the surface. If you eat too much baby aspirin, you get a ringing in your ears. I don't suggest trying it, but my friend did and said she sort of changed into somebody else until it went away.

Last year a meteor smacked into Siberia. I heard about it on the radio, how all those Russians were so efficient and replaced the glass in their windows within twenty-four hours. Would you expect it to be any different? Afterward, people scrambled to pick up remnants of that big rock to sell them—like it was London Bridge or The Berlin Wall. When we look at clouds in the sky, lying on our backs looking up, it's the shapes we tend to name. *That one looks like an elephant*, we say. Now it's changing into a heart. It helps us forget who we are, lets us <u>be</u> the imagining.

Surprisingly, I think of these random facts when I remember my cancer diagnosis. Whether we like it or not, there is a randomness and an intrigue to a diagnosis. Doctors practice medicine, they don't perfect it. And a diagnosis is a story, a kind of script to help everyone involved navigate the way. It is a guess, a best guess, but a guess all the same. But it is more than factual, more than one dimensional. It changes everything in an instant and for good. For the patient, it grows tentacles, weaves its way into all elements of the life. It has no beginning and no end. It is colossal and uncontainable.

There are days when I wonder if my cancer diagnosis was correct. What if it were somehow wrong? What if the biopsy was incorrect? The weeks surrounding it were mystical, filled with a kind of wonder. I lived in an altered state. This makes me remember that before Hippocrates came on the scene, epilepsy was considered the sacred disease. People thought it was brought on by the gods, thought the uncontrollable moving of the arms and legs, the fixed staring, were divine. But the father of medicine, Hippocrates, declared it no more sacred than other diseases. But note that he did not dismiss sacredness altogether. He simply said it was not more sacred. This puts all disease into the sacred category. And I tend to agree. When ill, don't we feel changed, a bit otherworldly, stricken, taken over?

In the initial meeting with the surgical oncologist, a humorless man from Indiana, I was handed a three-ring binder, the bulk of which I'd not seen since undergraduate microbiology class. And though I was sure this man would never laugh, he did grant me permission to throw the thing in the dumpster the moment I exited the hospital, said that was an option of something to do with it. Instead, I went home and spent a long night reading all that was going to happen to me: radical mastectomy, chemotherapy, radiation. I sat on the checkered couch my friend Jill had given me, and it felt like I was reading about what was going to happen to someone else, someone I only vaguely knew. It was not until the next day that I realized this was going to involve me.

The surgery was long, lasting five full hours. In the recovery room, friends who'd come to be with me said the surgeon looked exhausted when he left the operating room. He told me I had a lot of muscle, which made it hard to remove the breasts. In surgery, there were six people, including the surgical oncologist and the plastic surgeon. They took out my sentinel lymph node, found it to have cancer, and removed sixteen other nodes, six of which were cancerous, putting me at stage three.

Gordon Morris was my medical oncologist, the man who'd be with me for the next five years, overseeing my chemotherapy. The handmade sweaters he wore, ones patients had made him over the years, were bright and cheerful and gave the impression that we were on a family ski trip, not taking white blood cells counts every few days. His "uniform" was a pair of suspenders someone had needlepointed for him with miniature scenes of cows grazing, of fly-fishing, of daffodils, and of a pewter mug of beer.

Once I'd recovered enough after surgery, a couple of weeks, Gordon ordered what he called *the big guns*, strong chemo because he said I could take it, because that would be powerful and get the cancer. What struck me was that all those drugs had the letter x in them: Taxotere and cytoxin, startling names, disconcerting words. Why, I thought, not just name them after doves or homing pigeons who can reliably find their way back after a journey?

I was trooping along pretty well, two chemos down when he told me that the concoctions they were giving me would put me through menopause. Well, that was a shock: overnight menopause. We needed that, he explained, because the estrogen was food for my cancer. I remember pulling the hospital gown over my head to hide my crying. This was too much, I thought, reminding me of Kipling's elephant's child on the banks of the Limpopo, *that was just too much to take.*

Gordon was a true artist. He cared more than was good for him. He saw his patients as people, as his flock, in the very best way. He took on the job of physician, counselor, friend, alchemist, even adoptive uncle to Emma and Garland. They were seven and four at the time, and he'd hand them a few dollars and escort them to the cafeteria when I came to chemo so they wouldn't be present in the room when a nurse started the IVs.

Because the chemo was depleting my white blood cell count, I had to take the drug Neulasta. You've likely seen the adds, white kitchen with a porch out onto a manicured lawn equipped with a golden retriever, a 60-something cancer patient and his or her spouse. Today you can get a Neulasta patch, but in 2005 the drug was still patented, not yet generic. If I got the shot at the hospital, it would cost me $800.00 out of pocket each time. So, Gordon scheduled my chemos for Friday, and the next day, Saturday, when I needed the shot when he was off work, he'd meet me at the local high school where he would administer it to me. I now realize he must have pilfered, or paid for himself, that Neulasta. I'd hop into his truck, he would give me the shot, and we'd both be off on our way.

When my period came back, six weeks after the last chemo, rather than telling me in the office what needed to be done, he said, *Miss Charlotte, let's go for a walk.* We got in the elevator and rode it up and down, up and down what must have been eight times while he let me cry. Tomorrow, I've ordered for you to have an ouverectomy to, as he said, *whip those bad boy ovaries out.* They were feeding the cancer and needed to go.

I threw myself a kind of party a week before the third chemo, the one they said would cause my hair to fall out. My friends and I ate pasta, drank wine, and cut off chunks of my hair, leaving me with a real cute pixie. Six months later, that spring, one friend wrote me a letter to say she'd taken some of my hair to the grove beside her pasture and placed it on a willow branch. She reported that a bluebird had made her nest partly of my hair. She even saw the bird flying with some chestnut hair in her beak: my hair in the beak of a bird, en route to making a home for offspring. What all this did to Emma and Garland I'll never know. It hurts me to think of it except when I see Garland skateboarding down a hill, all sureness and grace, I know it did not come to him as easily as it looks.

surprising people my mother admired

My mother openly venerated the woman who kept all she owned in a grocery cart. The times we'd pass her in the car, pass her post on the corner of McArthur Boulevard near Sibley hospital, Mommy would say she envied her freedom, how she was unbound from the confines of family, how she could come and go as she wished. *And think how much time she has for reading*, she would establish. At the public library, where Mommy volunteered, she could turn into somebody else, someone content, as she shelved the books, lined up the spines, made sure the stories were arranged just as they should be. I bet she got a little nervous when people checked out books like she was unsure of where they were going. She loved books that much.

You might remember the Scarsdale diet, one of the first ever low carb diets a Dr. Herman Tarnower created. Well, his lover, who happened to also be the headmistress of The Madeira School, killed him. And my mother had lunch with her, with Jean Harris, a few hours before she drove up to Purchase, New York state and shot him. When Mommy came in the house after that lunch, she looked flustered, not herself. When I asked her what happened, she was hesitant at first, then reported that Mrs. Harris seemed out of sorts, that she seemed agitated. My mother felt that she was going to do something rash. And that she did.

The New York Times reported that Ms. Harris drove from Virginia to Dr. Tarnower's *place so she could have a few quiet moments with him before she shot herself 'at the side of the pond where there were daffodils in the spring.'* But instead of killing herself, she killed him after seeing another woman's bra on his bed. Jean Harris spent most of the rest of her life in prison where she organized a library and tutored inmates, set up a nursery for children born to inmates. My mother assiduously followed the story. I have a suspicion that she saw herself in this woman who was self-assured and independent, who took her circumstances and made something of them. I know my mother had that in her, too, know that if she had to serve time, she, too, would help the women with her obtain their GEDs.

bedazzlement

If forced to name a favorite indoor space, I would choose the greenhouse at The National Cathedral, pure bedazzlement. The first thing to love is the humidity of the place, particularly on a grey February day. The top panes of glass are full and solid, and the sides have cantilevered panes. On the left-hand bench are dozens of green foliage plants: baby's tears and ferns and moss. It's enough to bring you back to your moorings, the smell of dirt and live growing things. There are orchids and lilies and bonsai, strange small worlds unto themselves. The floor is of pea gravel and gives a bit when you walk, takes you back to the seaside. In middle school and high school, I'd walk up there most weekends and spend my allowance money on a plant. I'd walk the aisles, taking in the smells and the life.

When I go back to our nation's capital, the city of my youth, I always visit the cathedral. The peal of the bells is so sweet and carries so far I want to tell my mother about it. I want to tell her they are playing rounds at eight. But she's gone. Except I detest that euphemism. Gone? Gone where? And even worse is passed on. *Sarah passed on.* Makes it sound so intentional like that's how she planned it in the way she might have planned to take a cruise. Let's just say it. *She is dead. She died.* My mother is dead. And I hate it that's so. But here is something. Before I sold the house, I went through her belongings. Emptying her dresser, I found she'd saved my baby teeth in an amber prescription vial. On the label, in tiny cursive—the date I'd lost each one. Just maybe I was what she'd wanted after all.

When I'm not writing or thinking about writing or cleaning the kitchen for the fifth time of the day to avoid writing, I go to the rec center. It's a two-story affair with a kind of balcony of stationary bikes and stair-masters and ergometers and treadmills. Once I get my body over there, I spend much of my time under the delusion that I'm 22 again, back in college. I look at the other humans in this space, and they are 22, so why can't I be? Just a couple of hours ago, I got on a treadmill next to a kid who must have been on some kind of varsity team: the cut-off shirt, the way he carried himself. Well, I just thought I'd go ahead and compete with him. Because he was plugged into his iPod, I felt certain he wouldn't notice when I kept on looking over to his screen to see what speed he had his treadmill set to. So, I upped my machine to match his until I literally started seeing stars and had to go back to my regular 10-minute mile. That felt bedazzling for sure.

But the word bedazzlement makes me remember Bertha Lee Morris, Lee Lee as we called her. She canned beans, and she shelled black walnuts. She took in stray dogs and other people's children. When she kept Garland, she'd make him homemade French fries every day. He'd toddle up to her chair—she was in her late seventies then—and hand her a baking potato. She'd get herself up, go to the kitchen and cut that potato into perfect strips. Next, she's put tablespoons of Crisco into the cast iron pan. While it was melting, she'd pat the potatoes dry with such affection it looked like she had just bathed a puppy. Not until the potatoes were in the pan would she begin singing. And it was usually a hymn or another song from church. She often sang *I'll Fly Away*. She'd almost croon *one bright morning when this life is over*. How dazzling she was in her feed sack dress and apron, her grey hair done up in long braids. Just think of all we know but cannot see: God, of course, but also time and magnetism, sound and oxygen, longing, kindness, distance, and fear.

Before she took in children, she worked third shift at Conagra putting turkey into the frozen dinners, or what we used to call T.V. dinners. She needed that job but was not ever going to go against what she knew to be right. One day she noticed that the chunks of white meat did not seem fresh, so pulled the cord that summoned the line chief, her boss. She pointed to the vat of meat and said, *this meat is soured, we shouldn't put it in the trays*. When he told her that she was to go ahead and put the customary two scoops into the reservoir of each black plastic tray, she said she would not. When he told that would cost her her job, she took off her apron, her hairnet, and quit right then and there. Dazzling, brave Lee Lee.

Lee Lee died on Good Friday on her 91st birthday. What are the odds of that? I'll tell you. I looked it up. Good Friday fell on her birthday when she was 7, when she was 17 when she was 29 but not since then. And she was devout beyond devout. She read the Bible with such ardor it sometimes seemed she was afraid it would cease to be, that she needed to take every chance she could to nourish herself in its lessons and stories. It was, actually, the only thing she ever read.

We buried her in a graveyard where most every stone had the name Morris or Shifflett or Chisholm, families who've lived in these Virginia hills a very, very long time. People joke that the names are so common because everyone's related to each other. And while that may have some truth to it, I choose to honor them and the fact that they've stayed where so many of us have come in and taken over their land. I didn't go to family night, but the graveside service was horrific. The preacher called her Sister Lee and kept on insisting she'd gone on to better places where the streets are lined in gold. Clearly, he barely knew her. She had never driven a car, never had a license, so when her husband Lester died a decade before her, she no longer attended Church of The Brethren. But boy-oh-boy, he talked as if they'd spent every afternoon sitting on a porch swing side by side. He had no facts about her life, no feeling for who she was, just assurance that now she would not be subject to all the pains and sorrows of this life. Driving home from it, I told Emma I wouldn't ever want to live in a place with streets lined in gold; it would get awfully hot, after all. And be hard on the eyes. Lee Lee wouldn't like it either.

Definitely in the category of bedazzlement would fall my former landlord, Jacob Elwood Hall. After college, a friend and I rented a house in Boonesville from him on his farm of over a thousand acres. To supplement our small rent, we helped feed out cattle in winter and get up hay in the summer and fall. During a wet summer, there would be three good cuttings. The smell was luscious. After the haybine cut the grass, it would be mowed into neat windrows all along the field. Then the baler would chug through and pack the windrows into square bales, then spit them out, kahplop. This is where our work came in. Dressed in long-sleeved shirts and blue jeans, with bandanas around our necks to keep from getting scratched, we'd hoist the bales onto the truck bed. Later, we'd bring the hay to the barn to stack it neatly in rows. In winter, we fed the hay to his Herefords and black white face cows.

Mr. Hall and his wife, Nellie, kept a garden back of the house we rented. Some afternoons they would work the soil together, putting in the glorious seeds. He'd whistle and take the blunt end of his rake to make a perfect hole, and Nellie would drop the corn kernel or green bean seed, tamping it down with her hands. Late in his life, Mr. Hall would wander into our house without even knocking. He'd make himself comfortable on the couch. I'd bring him a glass of water, and we'd sit together, him whistling a church hymn.

things that hide in plain sight

In her book *The History of Love*, Nicole Krauss writes, *the stone of the wall that separates me from childhood began to crumble at last*. The stone of the wall: how accurate, how well I understand those words. Don't a great majority of us build just such a wall, fortress of protection. We need it, I think, for well over a decade after leaving home. It lets us differentiate our newly grown selves from our childhood ones. Otherwise, it is all just too much to bear. What did you learn too early? What do you wish you didn't know?

For me, childhood shared many of the peculiarities of a wall of mirrors. At a carnival sometimes you'll find one, a series of passageways lined with mirrors, everything distorted. And much like a carnival, a wall of mirrors confuses. There are competing versions of reality. Yes, that's it: competing versions of reality. There was the version we spoke. There was the version we thought as individuals. And they were in direct conflict. We ate dinner at exactly 7:15 every night so we could at least say we ate dinner together. But there was nothing honest about that time together. We were listening to what each of us did not say, to what we withheld. Flannery O'Connor reminds us that anybody who has survived childhood has enough to write about for the rest of one's days. How true that is.

When I think of my phone number growing up, 202-338-0101, I briefly flirt with the idea of dialing it. But the obvious hazard is what if someone answered who was not my mother? And the probability of that is quite high, almost 100%. The black phone sat on a stand of its very own in the hallway. The stand had a pad of paper and a pen so you could leave a message for someone, or jot down notes. It, too, was black, lacquered and shiny and flawless. You know how you can only see fireflies after dark? That's how I think of the phone, not a relic from the past. It's still there in the front hallway waiting for a call to come in.

past activities

My father taught me how to shoot a gun, his Winchester Model 70. He would balance a tomato sauce can on a fence post, label still on, and teach me to steady myself, teach me to focus. It had to do with breathing, he explained to me. But all I could envision was the sauce can, afraid it would fall off the fence post before I even got my chance to pull the trigger. We'd do this on Saturdays, and the gun's report was so loud I'd surprise myself, the way a dog does sneezing, the way they'll look up at you as if to ask, *what just happened?* I have no memory of how well I did, how many cans I successfully hit. But do remember the shredded labels, Heinz Tomato Sauce turning spectacularly into *He Too Sau.* I thought it was a secret message from afar, thought maybe God was saying He also saw what I'd done.

I like choices, the fact that I get to choose what I wear, what direction I walk in, what pen to employ. Choices are a gift, except when there get to be too many, as is the case in the cereal aisle. But that is another story, the less said about it, the better.

As a child, I thought people would go and die on purpose in the manner they would go on a vacation. The one time I remember my parents going on vacation together, I must have been eight and though I have no idea where they went, what I do remember was when they came back. And I thought that games were realer than real. Bombardment was a game we played in gym. Like dodgeball, the point was to avoid being hit, the ball one of those ubiquitous orangish playground balls. Maybe all that was different from actual dodge ball was that we hit each other hard, intentionally, and then sent one another to jail which was the area behind the basketball hoop on the other team's side. The way to get out of jail was if one of your own teammates managed to hurl the ball all the way into the jail and you caught it. What's strange, writing this, is how well I remember the game, as if were happening now.

My mother was both near-sighted and astigmatic. She wore thick glasses all the time. Most often in the car, at a stop-light, she would take off her glasses and breathe on the lenses to fog them up, then wipe them clean with a corner of her shirt or jacket. Then she'd sigh, a kind of satisfaction sound, and replace the glasses just in time for the light to turn green.

Whenever my mother adopted another dog from the pound, she'd spend days mulling over what to rename it. She felt this important, said that to name something is to give it a new life. She walked about the house testing out the name to see how it echoed off the plaster walls. Once, I remember her boiling water and while the kettle's whistle resounded, she recited choices of dog names into the increasingly humid kitchen. She explained that a dog's name must be easily recognizable to the dog, no Jeffrey or Zooey, nothing too complex. How she knew this, I don't know, but I believe her. She said that the name Molly wasn't a name a dog would readily respond to. And this is when she came up with the self-imposed rule that all the dog names had to begin with the letter A: Agatha, Asia, Annie.

magnificent inventions

•——————————————→•

Let's begin with the shoe horn. Those are the devices that help you slip your heel into your shoe without having to tussle with it much. And I found out that you can buy a solid gold one from Tiffany's for nine thousand dollars. But I digress. Think of all you could do with a shoe horn. It could be a spoon for the quart of ice cream you want to eat rather expeditiously in the wee hours of the night. It could be a shovel for planting petunias.

Then, of course, we have metal gadgets used for measuring feet, which are called Brannock devices. The guy who invented it, Charles Brannock, made the first one out of an Erector set. Before he patented it in the early 1900s, people's feet were measured using a block of wood, which, of course, does not work as well. It cannot be manipulated. How cold the metal of the Brannock device felt beneath my thin white bobby socks. We were in the store because my Stride Rites had gotten too snug. And there was always the moment of truth: had my feet grown? If so, would I grow more? It felt triumphant if I'd moved even a half size up. And my mother seemed so proud like we'd both done something rare to make this happen.

Life's great mysteries. Here's one: a sticker of captain marvel on the pineapple I bought yesterday. I could understand it being on a banana, but a prickly fruit? How does the sticker even stick, even stay put? So much is just flat out strange. Scouring Craigslist, doing anything to avoid sitting down to write, I found a listing for fainting goats. And I took a moment to think that one through. Goats are terrifically smart. In college, I had a job milking Nubian goats at a local farm a few times each week. There were four milking beds and twelve goats, and they knew their milking order. When my car pulled up beside the barn, the ladies would line up: Athena, Clarissa, Helena, Clarice, all twelve of them in the correct order. This must have been the kind of wondrous phenomenon Gerard Manley Hopkins had in mind when he wrote Pied Beauty: *whatever is fickle, freckled who knows how. Whatever is spare, strange original. All their gear and tackle and trade. Praise him.*

Remember when bead stores were all the rage? And places where you could paint mugs and casserole dishes they'd fire for you? Well, those have gone the way of the masked boogie bird. But there are still homing pigeons, wondrous creatures. Those guys and gals will fly clear across the ocean to make their way home. A student once brought two of hers into class for her final project. We all traipsed outside after her. She opened their carrying box and then skyped her husband at home, thirty miles away. Twenty minutes later, we watched as they made their safe arrival back to their coop on their farm. The final wonder I'll add to this list is recordings of people laughing during a comedy routine. They sound euphoric, spun out of control, and there is almost always one person whose laugh is so outrageous it makes you laugh just listening to it.

Did you know that the word strangely contains the word angel? The word strange comes from a French word that once meant distant and inhospitable. And that strikes me as the opposite of angelic. To help you contextualize, let me tell you a story. There is a famous jockey named Angel Cordero. When Clark graduated from Skidmore College in Saratoga Springs, New York, Mommy and I went to the flat track. We miraculously found ourselves mere feet from Angel as he stood preparing to mount Gate Dancer. Instead of blandly walking up to her and getting on, he stood directly before that great beast and looked her in the eye for a good long time. Then he kissed the middle of her forehead and crossed himself. Mommy and I stood in awe for what we had just witnessed.

Since we are onto the subject of horses, I'll share a few stories of my own. I used to ride, quite a lot. I worked at farms in exchange for time riding. I gave lessons and took lessons. Until the day I brazenly got aboard a racehorse on the flat track. It was a training track, one mile around. What I didn't know was that the way to slow such a horse is to use your weight, not the reins. When racehorses feel pressure on the bit, they are on high alert. And this one was going full speed, was at the gait called running which is faster than galloping.

She ran five times around that track, five miles. People in the barn came out and threw blankets at her hooves, trying to get her to stop. Which she finally did after running herself lame. It was absolutely terrifying. Since then, I have gotten on a horse, but not with the kind of pleasure I once had.

And there have been seriously sad moments. Once time a mare foundered in a field. It was the quietest thing I have ever seen. Her two-week-old foal bent over Molly who lay still the middle of the pasture. Hours earlier, she'd nibbled sweet feed from the palm of my hand, and I'd led them both out to graze under the cedars along the fence line. From the barn's door, I watched as her foal circled her body, reached his velvet muzzle to hers, pawed at her with his front hoof over and over to get her to get up. For a few moments, all was stock still, and I disappeared into myself wanting to unbelieve what I knew to be true.

directions for the hampster sitter

Instead of leaving a list of what plants to water and how to unlock the back door, I decided to leave a long-winded letter for our teenage neighbor who's taking care of things while we are at the beach. Here it is:

Dear Liza,

Besides all the obvious things (changing the shavings and making sure she's got food and fresh water) the problem you'll have is Andromeda knows far more than we want her to. When she looks out the window for the rain, it means the barometer has dropped. So, she'll know why you're feeling glum a full hour before you do. I'd suggest checking out the barometer, magnificent invention that it is, on the kitchen wall before you even attempt to go upstairs and deal with her. Next, of course, is the fact that she's duplicitous, full of guile. She'll throw you for a loop when you least expect it. Real clever. Just last week as I'm merrily getting ready to give her some time in her translucent exercise ball, she up and scoots between the mattress and the box spring. She has a healthy amount of free will. I had to take the entire bed apart, close the door, and wrangle the children to help me corner her. How's that for a head's up?

By this point, you are likely rolling your eyes and thinking this is the last time you will take on this job, that you have larger worries, like your upcoming

AP exams. But take a moment to consider the fact that hamsters are close relatives of the squirrel. When President Nixon made peace with the Chinese, they gave the National Zoo a pair of black squirrels, never before seen in the United States. It was all joy for a short time until the prolific mating abilities of squirrels revealed themselves. Now, when you go to our Nation's Capital and see a black squirrel, you'll know from whence it came. The days I don't want to feel invisible, I think of them, how they stand out with little way to hide. So, this is vital work, my dear hamster-sitting neighbor. I promise to pay you handsomely, and I promise, too, that your AP exam flashcards will still be there when you get home. Thank you for looking after Andromeda. We sincerely appreciate it.

I think of this when I consider Emma's job as an emergency room tech. Besides telling me about all the fascinating devices they have, the forceps and suture trays and premade splints, she explains the best way to start an IV line. She explains that not everyone's veins run the same way. And that you find the vein by feel and not by sight. Sight doesn't tell you the truth, she says. And I think how this is fitting for so much of life. Why is it that we ask how another person looked? *How did she look?*, we ask of our friend we haven't seen or of our colleague who is out sick. Well, they may look like death warmed over, but isn't it how they feel and how their heart is that holds the greatest import. I think Florence Nightingale, the lady with the lamp, understood this most decidedly.

right of way

Sailboats have right of way over motor boats. At a four-way stop, the vehicle on the left must yield the right-of-way to the vehicle on the right. Passenger trains have right of way over freight trains. Trains carrying people go faster. According to popular opinion, the Titanic was a magnificent invention before it took that nose dive. But what if that's not right? What if the passengers dressed in sequins and pearls were filled with a kind of knowing, the kind you have at a wedding you are sure won't last past the first year?

Did I say all this makes me think of my mother? By now, you're likely not surprised. She peoples my mind for large swaths of time most every day. You might mistake my dedication to her as melancholy. But this is not a fictional story. This is real life. If only she could have lived until her seventies. And how magnificent if she had taken up a musical instrument, something complex like the piccolo. But in my mind, she is the way she was. Most often, she is sitting reading a murder mystery. She believed in intrigue the way some people believe in God.

Sometimes when she comes to me, she is ironing, uninterrupted, no news on the radio, no Scott Joplin on the 8-track. Just my mother pressing the shoulder of one of my father's shirts. She has the shirt draped over the narrow end of the board and is moving the iron slowly, steam rising in great puffs, putting her in a cocoon of humidity.

Other times she is looking up a word in the OED with its teensy-weensy font that requires, terrifically, a magnifying glass—one that comes housed in a drawer in a box along with the two-volume set, the drawer with its very own grosgrain ribbon pull. The instant she understands how a word wended its way into its today-meaning, she lets out the breath she must have been holding, then hums and shelves that stalwart book.

A broken box, a dandelion, a stick of bamboo: all fragile and likely to get passed by, to be disregarded. When a bat found its way into our house, my mother did not panic. She called me at college to say it was there, said it the way she might report on the new novel she was reading. The bat had taken up residence in my childhood bedroom. And she was worried about what it could possibly find to eat, was convinced it would die of dehydration if she didn't do something to help it. I didn't ask her about it on the next phone call, figured it had found its own way out a window. But when I came home a few weeks later, leaning against my closet was the contraption she'd made to rescue and set free the bat: a broomstick with a coat hanger bent in a circle duct-taped to the end. Using binder clips, she'd attached a pillowcase to the coat hanger, making a kind of net. She must have been proud of that invention, her homemade bat catcher.

stiff as a board, light as a feather

This is what we said in high school when we tried levitation. We'd remind whatever girl who lay between us to make herself this way. Earlier, we'd walked to the Lucky 7 convenience store to buy cigarettes which we smoked in our dorm's dark basement. Boarding school is a strange arrangement, everyone with a discrete reason for being there.

To whistle FIRE in Morse code blow two shorts, one long then one short for F followed by one short for I followed by a short /long for R and two shorts for E. Garland taught me his when he was eight. He also told me that he wished to have yellow curtains in the windows of the treehouse we someday hoped we might build. Then he said, completely out of the blue—as the magnificent things children say so often are—*courageous people are everywhere mowing their lawns and ordering pizza.* Well, that kind of blew me away. And it also moved me. Sometimes it takes tremendous courage just to get through the day.

When I worked at a small Quaker school, one of my responsibilities was to serve as chair of what we called The Spiritual Life Committee. I remember little of what my responsibilities were except to start all faculty meetings with a few minutes of silence and to try to explain to new students that it's okay if you don't know the answer to a question. I also would remind my fellow teachers to *see the light in others and treat them as if that is all you can see.*

But one day stands out. The school was expanding and undergoing construction for a new science building. For weeks on end there had been a bulldozer outside humming and scraping, digging the foundation. When it abruptly stopped, break in the constant noise, I felt such relief until the principal came to my classroom and asked me to go talk to the bulldozer operator. Apparently, he'd unearthed something disarming. When I went outside, I saw a burly man walking in frantic circles talking on his cellphone. When he saw me approach, he ended his phone call, and together we peered into the massive hole he had been long at work on.

About a foot to the left of the bulldozer's blade was a wooden coffin, cracked upon. And sloshed out in the mud and dirt beside it was a human skeleton draped in black silk. It looked otherworldly, stunning, something Ansel Adams would photograph, the stark contrast of black material and white bone. The bulldozer operator, whose shirt informed me his name was Marshall, had resumed his circle pacing, repeating over and over: *I told her I was done. I. Am. Done. I cannot and will not do this one more minute. I am done for once and for all. I am done.* So, I solemnly nodded, half out of fear and half empathy, even though I had no idea what to do next.

It was as if he and I were standing vigil, our job to preside over this body. She was, for that time until the police came, our responsibility, so I decided to give her a name, Margaret. *Margaret, I am sorry your wedding dress blackened over these past one hundred years. Margaret, you are stiff as a board and light as a feather.* After the police arrived, and we answered their questions, Marshall left the bulldozer, left the shovel and the pickaxe, and walked got back in his Toyota to never return again. The history teacher and I took a sample of the woman's dress and had it dated. We reburied Margaret under the lilacs at the property's edge. And Marshall? I never saw him again. But I know that this is not what he needed to encounter. Certainly, running a bulldozer comes with its own set of risks, but a woman sloshing out in of a coffin dressed in her blackened wedding dress is not one of those.

negative capability

I'm taking care of my neighbor's horses while she's on vacation. She got three, pretty standard in size if you ever think of a horse as standard, but her husband's got a pair of Clydesdales. It's late June, and there's been mostly rain all month, so the flies are out something fierce. In the afternoon heat, flies gather in the corners of the horses' eyes and just about drive them crazy. If you've never seen a horse mask, it resembles the kind used in the sport of fencing except the horse masks' screens are made of fabric, not metal.

After I mask the three "standard" sized mares, I recognize there is no way in the world I am going to be able to reach even the withers on the Clydesdales. So, I search around the barn until I find a step ladder. Like most gigantic mammals, these beasts exude mercy. And they all wait ever so patiently as I stand atop the stepladder and velcro the masks under their chins, around their ears. Afterward I say the words *fly-masked Clydesdales* and put them out to their pasture to graze.

In the eye doctor's waiting room, the boy sitting next to me is talking to the images in the coloring book, a picture of three seals balancing beach balls. He's telling the seals he is there to brighten their day. He points with his index finger to the one on the far left, then turns to me and asks if the ball should be yellow or red. Wishing I had an instant opinion, I pause and then ask him which one he thinks it should be. Next, he tells me all about his gym class, how they have four colors of balls, two teams and play a version of bombardment, as far as I can tell. By now we're friends, this boy and me. And all of this is made possible by the fact that what looks to be his grandmother is ensconced in a copy of *Good Housekeeping*. She's got on her reading glasses and has created a bubbled world of her own.

The boy—Daniel I find out—is in this office to get glasses of his own. He's going to choose ones that make the seals come alive, he tells me. I love this about kids, how they are so certain. Adulthood tends to strip us of pluck and mettle, or maybe it's adolescence that does that trick. Either way, we lose assuredness that we innately have veracity, that we are owners of truth. Here's an often-told story, but it fits well here. A girl in kindergarten is drawing, bent over her paper, crayon clenched in her left hand. Her teacher comes up and asks, *Serena, what are you drawing?* Serena complacently establishes *God*. The teacher rebuts, *But, Serena, no one knows what God looks like.* And what is Serena's answer? *Well, now they do.* You just have to love that. Yesterday my plane had the first female pilot I've flown with, and it made me think of this story. Maybe the pilot was Serena, maybe she never lost her confidence. That's Serena over the plane's speaker proclaiming we are now at a safe cruising altitude.

Two Elderly Men Escape Nursing Home to Attend Heavy Metal Concert is the headline I read on the airplane. Let's picture them. There they are, their hearts unlearning the four walls, the games of Bingo, flaccid jello in pastel bowls, the way the nurses call them honey but don't mean it. They unlearn waiting for a son's visit, the calendar advertising what holiday's next, the overwrought decorations: all snowflakes and pumpkins and flags. They heard about the concert on the common room tv, looked each other square in the eye, grabbed their wallets and walking shoes, and got the hell out of dodge. By the time staff find them missing from their rooms, they are already halfway to that open-air concert where Judas Priest will remind them they might as well begin to put some action in their lives. And this they'll do, by golly, they'll feel, once again, the peculiarity of it all, feel themselves amidst the throngs of concert goers, right there with them, revived by explosive virtuosity.

We named the mixed breed we found in an alleyway Waif, and it fit him perfectly because he kept his ragamuffin appearance and temperament even after he lived snugly under our roof. He would sleep with one leg sticking straight up in the air like a flagpole. He would howl when an ambulance passed. He ate his food gingerly as if he were grateful for each and every bite, which is probably a good lesson for us all. He rode in the back of our doomed mustard-colored Buick and would bark at the mounted statues, and there was nothing you could do to stop him. He was convinced that they were real. Washington, D.C. has more equestrian statues than any city in the country, 29 to be exact. And Waif would bark at them with such ferocity you had to consider what was on his mind. His timbre was the same for George Washington as it was for Joan of Arc, resonance no louder for Don Quixote than Ulysses S. Grant. We suspected he saw something we could not. Which just maybe he did. Now, as statues are being pulled down and draped in black, I wonder if he was trying to point out what we were not yet willing to face.

Keats coined the term Negative Capability and proclaimed it to mean, "uncertainties, mysteries, doubts, without any irritable reaching after fact and reason." I translate that to mean it is the ability to hold two contradictory thoughts in your mind and not go crazy. Certainly, Waif had this very ability. He both believed the horses were real and that they were not. And the concert goers? They knew they'd eventually get caught, but for a few hours, they were going to let go of all fact and reason. Maybe negative capability is the fact two things can be true at the same time. Daniel in the waiting room: he believed he was bringing light to the seals' lives even though he knew they were images in a coloring book. And Serena, well, that was the way God looked to her.

practicing patience

My neighbor, Ian, has a part-time gig as a practice patient. It's at The University of Virginia Medical Center, which is a teaching hospital, and he is there to test how well the students diagnose symptoms he's made up. He'll feign abdominal pain, maybe even appendicitis, and see how attentively the medical students listen to him and if they figure out what to do with him. It's an honest-to-goodness paid job. It teaches students and interns techniques they need without having to subject an actual sick person to all the waiting and head-scratching. So, there's Ian lying on a gurney pretending his stomach hurts something awful when really he's feeling Jim-Dandy, couldn't be better. In fact, he just got back from a five-mile run, not an hour before dispatching himself to this gig.

From Ian, I learned that respiration and heartbeat are controlled by the medulla oblongata, the part of the brain responsible for involuntary reactions like sneezing and throwing up. But what I learned most is about bees. When he's not acting at the hospital, he is checking on hives for local beekeepers. My bees arrived in the mail, box the size of a shoebox. In it: 10,000 bees who'd journeyed together in a truck all the way from an apiary in Georgia.

In case you are not familiar with this, I will explain that bees arrive in the honest to goodness US mail in a screened-in box which contains workers and one queen. The queen is significantly larger—and more majestic, of course—

than the workers. She gets her own cage that is suspended within the larger package of bees. So, once the postmaster calls you to tell you to hurry on over and pick up your delivery, you transfer the whole kit caboodle to the hive you've assembled in your backyard. The queen stays in her cage and the workers, attracted to her, eat at the miniature cork that holds her in to release her. When my workers failed to get the queen out, I had to call upon Ian who came, not dressed in your usual beekeeping attire of a white zoot suit, but in shorts and a t-shirt. He said bees smell fear, and he had none. It was astounding to watch this thick set man so gracefully lift out a frame holding thousands of bees and set free the queen. My heart rate sure was up that day.

Thinking of Ian, I have set out to practice patience, not to be a practice patient. I start with my hive of bees whom I've become quite fond of. I like to sit on the grass about a foot from them and listen to their zipping around hard at work, keeping the queen warm and well fed. Sometimes I close my eyes and imagine I'm in there with them. I'm miniature and help them out a bit. It lasts a few good minutes, this envisioning. Later that day, back in the house, thinking of my bees, I practice patience with water. I get a little jar and fill it to the tippy top. I watch the light in the jar of water. At first, I place it on the windowsill, late afternoon, so it's half in shadow. But it's too plain, too even-tempered. In the bottle's water I place a little boat, small as a monopoly piece. And that seems to say part of what I'm after. A toy boat suspended in a jar of water. Next, I peel an orange in one long strip and place the curlicue next to the bottled boat.

teaching moments

In my freshman year of college, I took a class entitled Climates of Hunger. I chose it based solely on the name, far more interesting than Bio 101. These were the 80s in a big university, and there was no real advising to be had. The petite Indian professor stood at the front of the room every Tuesday and Thursday and explained in such a luscious way that when the high waters reached Punjab, they eroded the land, wreaking havoc. Everything he said made me want to lean back in my seat while we drifted together on a skiff, ventured out together to save those who had lost their homes and possessions.

While he lectured, I wrote poems about him. About what he wore. About how he was the first man I had ever seen who was even close to my height. How he was my father's age had my father still been alive. All semester there were no tests or quizzes, no papers, just his lectures, and my poems. It felt like I was going to a spa of words, a kind of enchanted story time. Until the final exam.

To prepare for it, I read over my notes thoroughly and felt ready to declare my knowledge of wind and rain and its power over human life. But instead of essays or short answers, the exam was filled with algorithms of daily mean rainfall and meteorological statistics, exclusively numbers. There were fill in the blanks and matching. And I had no clue as to the right answer for any of them.

When I got a 23 on the final and stood in line to talk to Dr. Thibou afterward, I overheard the hum of students around me sharing plans about summer internships at The Science Foundation and The Nature Conservancy. When it was my turn to speak to him, he was truly sorry that he hadn't noticed earlier, hadn't looked to see that I was an undergrad taking EnviSci 782, an upper-level graduate course.

But it was me who should have noted, on the first day of the lecture in Clarke Hall, that the other students were at least four years older than me. And I might have taken note of the syllabus. But I did not. Instead, I voraciously took notes as our professor explained how the monsoons created conditions that made it nearly impossible to grow food, how when the rainy season came, people starved. His accent and the way he talked with his hands enchanted me beyond belief. I never missed a class.

Dr. Thilabou was sincere and kind, and gracious. But it was too late to drop the class or claim some kind of special compensation. I showed him my notebook with the poems, and he was earnestly interested. But there was nothing either of us could do. That dropped my GPA significantly, but I remember it ever so well, and I remember his beautiful hands and his gentle ways. I did learn a great deal even if it's not reflected in my grade.

The hardest teaching job I've ever had was as a first-grade nap teacher. Yup, that's right, nap teacher. I was working part-time answering phones and logging in daily attendance at The Baltimore Waldorf School hoping with all my might that a teacher would call in sick one day, and I'd get my chance to be in a classroom, to sub for someone fighting the flu or a migraine. That day finally came one rainy October morning. The first-grade teacher was overburdened with her job, had too much on her plate. She needed someone to come in for 50 minutes every day after lunch and to lead what they called Nap Class. I was thrilled. I would get my hands wet, so to speak, would try teaching for a small amount of time.

Walking into that pristine, artful space with light pink walls, I was met by twenty children all sitting upright at their wooden desks with blankets and pillows in a neat pile underneath each chair. The teacher introduced me, and the children stood up in unison and recited, *Good Afternoon, Miss Matthews.* Well, that was a shock. *Why in the world are they doing this?* I thought. I felt myself starting to shake when the teacher slipped out unannounced, and I was suddenly in charge, or so I thought.

Twenty first-graders were staring at me. They stood upright behind their desks. They did not budge. For a full minute, it seemed, until I got up the courage to tell them they could sit down. Another minute passed, and a round-faced girl in the back row raised her hand and asked if they could make tents. I said yes and let me tell you, desks were being moved hither and thither, blankets flying, sudden bedlam. I was scared stiff. What if the teacher walked in to get her thermos of minestrone soup and saw this? What if I got fired on the first day? So, I garnered my courage and said in the strongest voice I could, *everyone, please stand still for a minute*. And they did. Bang. Just like that. Silence and stillness.

I told them that every other child could make a tent with his or her desk, but that it would have to be fast and quiet. Once they were all huddled in pairs under their desk tents, a hand shot up from under a gossamer blanket. I asked *yes?* And a high voice disappointedly said, *you're not playing the xylophone. Xylophone, xylophone*, I thought to myself looking around the room. Oh yes. So, I picked up the perfect wood, metal instrument and began banging away with the small mallet. Before even a minute had passed another hand shot up, *you're not playing Mother Earth*. Mother Earth? By the end of that nap time, I was huddled under a blanket myself, hiding. And a student in the front row was perched in the teacher's chair playing Mother Earth on the xylophone.

wonder of all wonders

When you can't sum everything up, sometimes it works to just give an image. As I noted earlier, my mother would bleed the furnace. This is advisably something you would get a skilled technician to do, but you can bet your bottom dollar that if my mother could do something herself, she would do it herself. And she even wrote it down, each October and April: *bleed the furnace.*

She'd emerge from the basement dressed in one of my father's work shirts smelling like oil and covered in red rust. One day I followed her down there and watched as she knelt and deftly wielded pliers being oh so careful not to over tighten the screw afterward lest she strip its delicate threads. It was magnificent watching her so capable in this task. Somehow, it reassured me that, despite everything, we were going to be alright. And that is something children desperately need to know. To this day, at the grocery store, when I inadvertently bump my cart into someone, and they forgive me by saying, *you're okay* I am eternally grateful. I am eight again. I am okay.

On the radio is a feature about bridge tenders, people whose job it is to open and close bridges so tall boats can pass under. The announcer labels it as a peculiar and slow-moving job. The interviewee is Maurice Little who tends the Grand Avenue swing bridge in Connecticut and waits all day for boats to come through: the coast guard, summer boaters. He can turn the traffic lights red. He says the trickiest part is getting the median lines back just right when he brings the bridge together again. I imagine it's a bit like trying to thread a needle when you do best if you look slightly to the side, not right at it. Another bridge tender in New Haven has become friends with the oystermen for whom he opens the drawbridge. Last week he invited Robert in for a beer, and they shared opinions about the tide. Both bridge tenders live in houses perched up high on cliffs. Boats call ahead when they want to pass. I can envision my mother doing that job too, bridge tending, imagining the lives of all who passed under in their boats. She's talking to herself about them at the end of a long winter day.

Bridges and trains are close cousins, so I will tell you a story about Emma. Last winter when the train carrying Republican lawmakers hurtled into a trash truck in the little town where I live, my daughter was the youngest first responder on scene. Emma's 19, new to this EMT gig. And she went right into the Amtrak cars to assess what needed to be done.

Wednesday is her shift day, 7:00 am to 7:00 pm, and she loves her crew. That's saying a lot. A whole lot. She's not the kind to make friends readily, keeps to herself with a few close confidants. Her temperament is earnest, even solemn. In kindergarten, the teacher's only concern about Emma was the fact that she didn't know how to do recess. She failed recess, the way Garland failed nap time. When all the other kids were blithely swooping on swings or bopping each other over the head with their lunch bags, Emma sat on an overturned log waiting to get back to business. She had her shapes to learn, after all, and the class hamster to hold. I've come to love this about her, how she's so intent, she has absolutely no tolerance for diversion. You can see it in her face and in the sometimes brusque way she moves.

On her crew is an ER nurse, a retired firefighter, an emigre from Istanbul, and the man she calls her new best friend. He's around 70 and comes into the squad house most days whistling. So far, he's taught her how to plumb a toilet, refuel the ambulances, fill oxygen tanks and grab her gear the instant the tone rings. Some weekends the crew will get together for a cookout or potluck. Her new best friend brings his dog, a dachshund named Bernard.

To watch Emma walk down the stairs on Wednesday morning feels the way it might for some when their daughter descents a winding stairwell all dressed for cotillion. Except Emma's got on the requisite blue cargo pants, blue collared shirt and the real-thing work boots with soles that help you not get electrocuted. In her pants pocket are two Sharpie markers, one pair of blunt scissors, and a penlight with a pupil gauge. In her jacket pocket is the super-duper stethoscope she paid for herself.

In coverage of the accident, we learn that more than half of the Republican members of the House and Senate were on board this charted train which was heading to the Greenbrier resort. We learn that it was a derailment. Meanwhile, the real Republican train wreck is happening right now in our nation's capital.

What we couldn't read about is how it felt. Or how it smelled, all that household trash newly strewn in a field. Or that the train was only partially derailed, so it was perilous to walk in the train cars, everything so unstable. How apt a metaphor this is for the state of our government. Clean-up crews have taken the train wreckage away. But there's still lots of trash. Lots of it. And there's a lone cross that lights up at night with a wreath of flowers encircling it—in memory of 28-year old Christopher Foley, the Time Disposal worker, who died. We can't dispose of time. We can't get rid of trash easily. We can't put back what's come undone. But I so wish we could.

As Emma maneuvered through the lopsided train car, a secret service agent stood in her way. He was thick and imposing with a clear, coil headset behind his ear. And she said to him, *I am going to count to five, and you are going to move out of my way.* That is what my daughter said to the man. And he moved. And she placed a cervical collar on the senator to stabilize his spinal column so he could safely be put on a stretcher and taken to help. If only she could do the same for our country.

Things of magnitude settle over you with excruciating slowness. It takes years to understand that all the moments of a childhood patch together to make a quilt that will accompany you all the days of your life: my mother playing with her dollhouse. Lately, I have tried to be watchful of the cows who live on the hill I pass on my way into town. They are Charolais— buttery in color with far-off sad faces. The herd stays together well, moving from spot to spot according to the grass. Their hill faces east and is rolling, dips so smooth they look as if they must be soft to touch if only they would shrink, or I grow, the proportions being wrong for the kind of touching I want. I have become interested in how they move. Walking downhill with their unwieldy bodies and four legs is both awkward and beautiful.

A few evenings back, just before full dark, the cows seemed restless, the way they get before a storm. But there was no storm and no apparent predator. They grouped close together in one of the middle creases of the hill, seeming to float for a brief moment as they neared the very center. Everything about them became liquid and strangely slow. It reminded me of the way they stand up next to one another in the hottest of August, swooshing the flies out of each other's faces, which my mother would have loved.

The first book I remember was Rachel Carson's *The Sense of Wonder*. While you are surely familiar with her book *Silent Spring* and its warnings about pesticide use, you may not have heard of *The Sense of Wonder*, remarkable book with charming black and white photographs. Carson was at work on it when she died of cancer at 56. It was published posthumously.

Here is my mother reading it to me: I'm wedged on the love seat next to her. She has *The Sense of Wonder* propped on a bolster pillow. She clears her throat and reads Miss Carson's words: *If I had influence with the good fairy who is supposed to preside over the christening of all children I should ask that her gift to each child in the world be a sense of wonder so indestructible that it would last throughout life, as an unfailing antidote against the boredom and disenchantments of later years, the sterile preoccupation with things artificial, the alienation from the sources of our strength.*

Now, my mother and I sit in silence for a few moments staring at the words on the page as if they might transmogrify, as if they might turn into something magical. Except they already have. Just listen to a few of them again: *If I had influence with the good fairy, I should ask that her gift to each child be a sense of wonder so indestructible that it would last as an unfailing antidote against the alienation from the sources of our strength.* Indeed, those are stunning, extraordinary words.

Next, my mother turns to look at me earnestly, asking with her expression what I, at the age of four, think about what she has just read. She wants to hear my thoughts on the matter. She explains that Miss Carson is my great aunt, and I should admire her. She explains that she accomplished what she did by paying attention, by noticing, by practicing patience. Miss Carson, she explains, spent whole afternoons at the edge of the sea collecting shells and mollusks, learning all she could with her hands and her eyes and her ears and her nose and her heart.

I am terror-stricken by what our species has done to this good earth. I am petrified by thinning ice, alarmed by worsening storm systems. My mother died because she played in contaminated dirt as a child. Of course, she didn't know it, nor did anyone who could warn her. But it was there, the poison, the arsenic that would kill her at the age of 62. Here is a poem about it:

The Year of Not Believing

My mother is six and does not know
what I have just read in the paper.
Kneeling in the backyard dirt,
she makes a fort for her doll Clara.
Her father's away on business so much
lately she's taken to spending early
evenings here, digging a world on her own.
Right now she's humming lullabies
so sweet I can hear them six decades later
in my chair, in my office, at this college
where each day I read The Washington Post,
where today's front-page story is about her
childhood neighborhood, a chemical
testing ground during WWI.
I call the Army Corps of Engineers because
that is what the paper said I could do.
Because that is all I can think of to do.
When I cite the slope of her backyard,
say her hematologist had never seen this leukemia,
not even in Nagasaki, not even in the worst of it,
I get hung up on. She died so suddenly
all I can picture is the oxygen mask fogging
because she was humming then, too.
She was still humming the sweetest tune.

But I am also given hope in the fact that earthquakes can turn water into gold. In the fact that baby saddleback tortoises have been found on the Galapagos Island of Pinzón for the first time in 100 years. As I read on the Internet this morning, "The tiny turtle find validates more than 50 years of conservation efforts." (Grenoble, 2019) And, after all, you and I are nothing more and nothing less than the interiors of collapsing stars.

When I asked Albert what thoughts he had about fear and what to do with it, he suggested facing it straight on. Start by looking at a picture of your fear several times each day and at unexpected moments. Yup. Just whip out that glossy photograph of a spider and stare at it for four seconds. Next, hold a plastic replica of it in the palm of your hand. I suggest even talking to it, making friends, so to speak. Then, watch a live one in a jar, get used to how it moves. Learn all you can about its ways. You might take a trip to the nearest reptile house and say to yourself: *behold, my fear is contained behind glass.* It is good advice for many circumstances.

To counter fear, let's include some birdsong. Listen for the winter wren with her bubbly cascading notes, for the mourning dove and his drifting coos that resurrect the long, outdoor days of childhood. Hear the wood thrush whose flute-like ee-oh-lay, ee-oh-lay reverberates through woods. Picture the barred owl who wondrously asks *who cooks for you? Who cooks for you?* Those sounds coming out of a heart-shaped face. Right now, outside my window, a chipping sparrow bops across the winter grass, so full of verve, its rusty head like a bouncing ball.

Emma's fallen into the good fortune of finding hearts most everywhere she goes. We'll be on a walk, gravel road, orchard to our right and she'll look down to behold a puddle in the shape of a heart. Yesterday it was a leaf on the windshield of her car: sycamore leaf, dappled yellow heart. And earlier in the week, a river stone. We keep what we can, the leaf and the stone, as reminders to have our eyes open for you might never know what you will stumble upon.

Because of this, as if it's something wondrously contagious, I've begun to spot hearts more often. At the beach, when we went last week, so many miniature pebbles in the shape of hearts. Sometimes you have to use your imagination, the sides of the heart not exactly the same in width or height, the groove between the two not perfectly a "v", but you can see it if you look it.

The opposite of fear might be finding heart-shaped leaves and birds' nests. I found one of those on the sidewalk outside the post office just yesterday. And then, the woman in front of me told the clerk she was there to pick up baby chicks, ones mailed to her from a hatchery in Iowa. When he set the box on the counter, their stalwart beaks poked through corrugated cardboard and chirping filled the room, floated over all of us waiting in line. Just like that and nothing's ever going to be the same. I tend to believe my own stories—the ones I tell myself. I'm terrifically gullible. Maybe this is one element cancer has taught me. You cannot think too much about what worries you, or you'll suffocate.

The thought of touching my mother still startles me. If I try to hold hands with Emma, she tells me she is busy, and we both laugh. We both laugh because she is not busy. We both know she is not busy, but it's okay. It brings to mind my mother's smell of soap and copper and leaves. I can see her in the living room, head supported by the side of her wing chair. I can see her reading. Later she is drafting a thank you letter as the cathedral's bells peal over the neighborhood. She is recounting the fact that all of us are nothing less than the interiors of stars.

acknowledgements

I offer grateful acknowledgement to the editors of the publications
in which parts of this memoir first appeared.

Book Mending
Five Points
Family Night
The Greensboro Review
Epoxy
Unicorn Press
First Hard Frost
American Poetry Review
My Daughter Gets Her Wisdom Teeth Extracted.
Blackbird
The Greatest Show on Earth
Virginia Quarterly Review
The Year of Not Believing
Virginia Quarterly Review
Variations on the Truth
Waccamaw
Whistle What Can't Be Said
storysouth

note from the author

Word-of-mouth is crucial for any author to succeed. If you enjoyed the book, please leave a review online—anywhere you are able. Even if it's just a sentence or two. It would make all the difference and would be very much appreciated.

Thanks!
Charlotte

about the author

Poet and professor at The University of Virginia, Charlotte Matthews treasures kindness and moss and miniatures. She is author of three full length collections: *Still Enough to Be Dreaming, Green Stars* and *Whistle What Can't Be Said*. Her honors include fellowships from The Chautauqua Institute, The Virginia Foundation for the Humanities and The Virginia Center for Creative Arts. She holds an M.F.A from Warren Wilson College's Program for Writers and a B.A. from the University of Virginia. She lives in Crozet, Virginia with her husband, two teenage children and a black lab named Linus.

Thank you so much for reading one of our **Biography / Memoirs**.

If you enjoyed our book, please check out our recommended title for your next great read!

Z.O.S. by Kay Merkel Boruff

"...dazzling in its specificity and intensity."

–C.W. Smith, author of *Understanding Women*

CPSIA information can be obtained
at www.ICGtesting.com
Printed in the USA
LVHW111526181219
640938LV00003B/466/P